# Hi, I'm Bill and I'm Old

"Funny, courageous, and empowering. In exploring the richness of his own life, William Alexander celebrates and invites us to discover the uniqueness and wisdom within ourselves. This book is a gift to those of us who are old, and even more, perhaps, to those who are young."

Zen Master Dennis Genpo Merzel, author of
*Big Mind, Big Heart: Finding Your Way*

"Moving between the intimacy of self-revelation and the universality of spiritual wisdom, Alexander takes us on an absorbing and illuminating journey to the outer edges of life."

Kevin Griffin, author of *One Breath at a Time:
Buddhism and the Twelve Steps*

# Hi, I'm Bill and I'm Old

## Reinventing My Sobriety for the Long Haul

William Alexander

## HAZELDEN

Hazelden
Center City, Minnesota 55012
hazelden.org

Library of Congress Cataloging-in-Publication Data

Alexander, Bill, 1942–
    Hi, I'm Bill and I'm old : reinventing my sobriety for the long haul /
William Alexander.
        p.    cm.
    ISBN 978-1-59285-663-3 (softcover)
    1. Older people—Alcohol use.    2. Older people—Drug use.
3. Alcoholism—Age factors.    4. Substance abuse—Age factors.
I. Title.
    HV5138.A44 2008
    616.86'06—dc22

                                                                2008029731

Editor's note
Alcoholics Anonymous, AA, and the Big Book are registered trademarks of
Alcoholics Anonymous World Services, Inc.
The names, details, and circumstances may have been changed to protect the
privacy of those mentioned in this publication.

12 11 10 09 08     1 2 3 4 5 6

Cover photography by Gene Bednarek, Southlight Photography
Cover design and interior design by David Spohn
Typesetting by BookMobile Design and Publishing Services

## To Lillis McElroy

Lillis was my paternal grandmother.
She was born in Center Point, Texas, on August 18, 1886,
and died in McKenzie, Tennessee, on June 24, 1976.
I didn't know until I was sixty-five years old that she was
the greatest influence in my life.

# Contents

# Acknowledgments

My thanks to the geezers in Gainesville and my compañeros in Costa Rica.

Three bows to the circle that surrounds me: Chris, Wendy, cousin Bill, Naomi, Masha, Sam, Haqiqa, Lenny, Mark, Gracie, Feral, Hugh, Evelyn, Claire, Pat, and Elene.

To my formal teachers: Khenpo Ugyen Tenzin, of Bhutan, who taught me that everything that happens in my life is a direct result of some action I have taken in the past, and Dennis Genpo Merzel Roshi, who showed this aging hippie that his inner competitor, disowned in 1967, was alive and well in the present moment.

Deep gratitude goes to Bill, Bruce, Courtney, and Steve, health care pros, one way or another, who have had the thankless task of protecting this aging man from himself.

I raise a glass to Paul Schaubel, without whom I'd have lost my way entirely.

Kamala and Will remain my greatest teachers. My gratitude and love floods their plains. And thanks to their mothers as well, Beverly and Pauline. And to Liz, Ed, and Johnny-Boy.

My brother, Phil, is as close to my heart as I've ever let anyone get. I'm a fortunate man.

Much credit goes to countless anonymice who showed

me the way, and especially to those who let me find it on my own.

Finally: The great gift of my struggles is Sid Farrar at Hazelden. He did what only my grandmother Alexander had done before. He saw through the confusion to the storytelling boy I once was, whom she saw and whom Sid set free. Not many authors can claim a spiritual relationship with their editors. I can. Lucky me.

# Preface

I have written this book for everyone who is aging or who hopes to age. There is emphasis on how aging affects those of us who have moved beyond substance abuse and addiction, but you will also find that I believe that most everyone, whether they use alcohol or other drugs or not, is addicted. Addicted, that is, to the chimera of a separate, freestanding, autonomous *self.* Walt Whitman knew well the process of curing off that small self when he wrote, "I know I have the best of time and space, and was never measured and never will be measured." I have measured myself, of course, for years, and it was only in my seventh decade that the tape began to break.

This story is entirely personal. I see sobriety as a radical way of living on this earth: endlessly honest, open, and willing. To reinvent my sobriety, it was necessary for me to review my life and "re-vision" my story—my self.

While I'm writing this book with older people in mind (and more specifically older people who have had histories of drug and alcohol dependence), if you are drug free and twenty-five or thirty-five or forty-five, this book is still for you. Elders are simply the gatekeepers and the guides to the territory ahead. Those who have died, at an old age, can show us a road we have yet to walk. So don't be put off by my use of the word *old* in the title.

This book is for anyone who ages. All of us, that is—or at least the fortunate ones.

You will not find information on health care options, retirement communities in Costa Rica (which all look like Santa Barbara South), or the pitfalls of failing prostate health. You will find that I have tried to reduce desire, live more simply, and practice noninterference; that I have a small rented home in a very primitive and "de-gringoed" part of Costa Rica; and that my bladder has finally given up, under the onslaught of years of drinking alcohol and mainlining caffeine, and it behaves however it wishes whenever it wishes.

This is not an "autopathography." You will not find tales of family dysfunction, stories about bizarre drug and alcohol use, details of my sex life, or *kumbaya* moments of spiritual elevation. I am not one for exhibitionism-by-proxy, and so my family and others are not trotted out to show how I've suffered. Many names are false, and a few places disguised. There is one fictional character. You'll probably recognize that one when she arrives, toward the end of the book.

In spite of my debilitating tendency toward name-dropping, you will find only one gee-whiz reference to the famed folk I have met. In order to save you the trouble of searching the book now, I will tell you that it is Phil Everly. (If you don't know who Phil Everly is, you might question whether this book is for you at all.)

I have nothing to say about conscious aging, ethical wills, or the Kevorkian option. You will not find economic speculation about the impact of the aging boomer generation, of which I am obdurately not a part. (I'm too old for that particular demographic, thank the gods, by about three years at this writing.)

Nor will you find cookie-cutter generalizations about aging.

You will find what turned out to be, much to my amusement, a somewhat narcissistic detective story. I ended up investigating a series of crimes I committed, ones in which I was not the only victim, but was often the principal one.

You will find my experience of finding my true self, protean in nature, emerging from behind the failing masks. A jester on horseback, according to my son. I miss the exuberance and juicy vanity of youth, so I'm leaving that description in. It's wrong, of course, but there it is.

You will also find that the title of this book is entirely accurate—that I am old—and that "old" is a very good thing to be, and a rare thing, not confined to chronological age.

So come along. That "long, strange trip" we've heard about? I found out that it's the trip home. And it isn't over—not by a long shot.

# Aging

> *"Old age is the most unexpected of things*
> *that can happen to a man."*
> —Leon Trotsky
> *Diary in Exile*

# Reverie: Oblivion

*The dead dark hangs outside of my closed curtains. After midnight the night is a presence, heavy and persistent. No sound, no movement, no smells or tastes of night. There is only darkness and a heavy weight.*

*I am drunk. After twenty-three years without a drink, I sit in my brightly painted den—with the masks I collected in Central America and Bhutan, the tangkhas from the Himalayas, the rubbing of the gravestone of Delta blues pioneer Charley Patton, and the pictures of my son—and I drift into oblivion.*

*The only light is from two Japanese lanterns in the corners. The quart bottle of Jack Daniel's is half empty. I hold the heavy crystal tumbler in my right hand, with a Camel straight perched between my index and middle fingers. The smoke drifts to the slow-moving ceiling fan. The drapes are closed against the night, and all is silence but the humming in my ears. I am alone and my dark twin has been fed at last. I have no responsibilities and I am free. No one knows where I am, and tomorrow I will be gone again. But right now there is no tomorrow. Only the dark and the stillness.*

*It is July 16, 2007, I am sixty-five years old, and I have not had a drink or wanted one since June 24, 1984. The wraiths have my mind, and ancient snakes have come alive in my belly. Oblivion, my first default. Drunk again.*

Not so.

It was a reverie, but by no means "mere." I shook it off. There was no bottle, no tumbler, no cigarette.

The date was indeed July 16, 2007, but the drapes were open, the night was fully present to me through the opened doors, and the tree frogs sang by the creek down the slope behind my house. I had been entranced, living in a vision of something that never happened. I don't know how long it lasted. It was a lie told by the mind of addiction, my dark twin, always with me, just behind and off to the left, sinister and leering, in shadows and mist, waiting. I had not had a drink in this house since June of 1984. I had never wanted a drink since that day. Drinking had never occurred to me, during good times or bad. Not for over twenty-three years.

Why now? My life was good. I had a nice home that I had just emptied of decades' worth of collected books, furniture, records, and CDs. I had unplugged my television set and put the books that remained after the great sell-off in my upstairs office. They were mainly books of poetry, largely Chinese, and some original texts of religions both from the West and East. There was some Florida history and, my favorites, the novels of Randy Wayne White and Ace Atkins. I was single. I lived with my cat, Fred, who's not a drinker. I had friends in this small town and more friends scattered across the planet. I was writing my first novel, set in China in the Tang Dynasty.

My seventeen-year-old son was in Maine, working at a camp he had attended during the fall semester of 2006. My health was good. My enemies list was empty, for the first time in several years.

What had happened?

I sipped iced tea (decaffeinated) and chewed on a piece of cold (vegetarian) pizza. I let my eyes roam the opposite wall, where they fell on a tangkha I had bought in Thimphu, Bhutan, in the fall of 1999, toward the end of a month-long trek in that unearthly Buddhist kingdom. A tangkha, loosely, is a scroll painting on a background of silk brocade, which always fulfills a spiritual function, often in temple ritual or meditation on the images. This one on my wall was a depiction of the Wheel of Life, the Tibetan image of the six realms of existence in the world of Samsara, or delusion. The image rests on a magnificent tapestry of green silk with starbursts of white and progressive borders of gold and red. The image is held in the jaws of the Monster of Impermanence, with his crown of skulls and rage-distorted red face.

My eye fell on two realms. The first, the Realm of the Titans, is the realm of those who fight the gods in pursuit of their own greedy aims and ambitions. It is the realm of endless war. I reflected briefly on my country, with sadness. Then I looked at the Realm of the Hungry Ghosts, with bloated bellies and necks too thin to admit the sustenance their greed demanded. They are never satisfied and can never be. I thought about myself.

Here I was, content, I reckoned, with a good life, and yet I was thinking, with longing, of drinking again. My life, and yours perhaps, is a life of perpetual longing and endless dissatisfaction.

Do I want more? Am I insatiable? No, I thought, I want less. I want the poems and the hot days, but all the old thrills are gone, thank the gods. Yet—wanting less is still wanting. Endless and pervasive dissatisfaction. In the parlance of Alcoholics Anonymous, I was restless, irritable, and discontented.

The night grew deeper and my mind came to a fitful rest, finally, in the deeply spiritual place of "don't know." I finished off the pizza, gulped down the final mouthfuls of the iced tea, cleaned the kitchen, gave Fred a good brushing, and closed the house down for the night. I climbed into bed, without reading from the ever-present novel by my bedside, in this case Randy Wayne White's *Sanibel Flats*. I lay there in the dappled dark. The frogs were in full throat. Time to sleep, the acceptable oblivion.

Nope.

Restless still, I got out of bed after only a few minutes, pulled on my black meditation robe, and went downstairs into my former living room, now an austere meditation hall, and arranged myself into sitting posture on the black meditation cushions beneath the bookcases.

Something was nagging at me. What is it?

In some deep-down place, I saw a Möbius strip of light, rotating in the winds of my mind, but it wouldn't hold still long enough for me to read its circular message. I finally nodded out on the cushion, jumped awake, startled, got up, stripped off the robe on my way upstairs, and hit the bed.

For the next three days, that "what is it?" was the subtext of my life, a current like some Florida rivers, sometimes on the surface, more often flowing below ground, below consciousness.

That weekend I called my friend Hugh, in Eugene, Oregon, known in some circles as "The People's Republic of Eugene," where Hugh and Evelyn are happily retired.

Hugh has been sober longer than Jesus, and has been a Zen student and practitioner for over thirty years as well. I told Hugh about the oblivion reverie, emphasizing that I didn't really want to drink, that I was just thinking about it. He understood that and put a sharper point on it. "You were speculating," he opined. That was it exactly. He asked what I thought might have been behind it, other than the obvious reality that I'm an alcoholic, and I went through the worn list that I had been carrying around for days—Will's away from home for the first summer ever, I'm worried about money, I broke a weekend date with a longtime lover and felt guilty, I was studying kung fu again and my hip felt like it was about to go out the way it did a year ago, I "should" be able to retire, and on and on. The list was probably as boring to Hugh as it was to me. It was a litany with content but no feeling.

When I stopped to take a breath, Hugh said, "You've told me exactly the reason and you haven't heard it, not once." OK, so tell me. He said that I prefaced nearly everything with "I'm sixty-five years old and . . ."

"You're getting old," he said, "and you don't want to."

Bingo. I recalled that at one point during the reverie I had thought, "OK, twenty-three years sober, I've made my point."

So here I was, powerless again, and in ways that I could not have imagined.

*Tell all the Truth but tell it slant—*
*Success in Circuit lies*
*Too bright for our infirm Delight*
*The Truth's superb surprise*

*As Lightning to the Children eased*
*With explanation kind*
*The Truth must dazzle gradually*
*Or every man be blind—*
—**Emily Dickinson**

# No Escape

Old age is the undercurrent of our lives. It cannot be denied, not really; it cannot be bargained with, and it cannot be resolved. Birth, sickness, old age, and death are the unavoidable realities of suffering, according to the Buddha. What a curriculum!

There is no con that will fool old age. I saw an ad recently for some injectable gel that would make the gel junkie look younger. The list of possible side effects was worthy of an essay by Steve Martin. Although "a desire to join a death cult" was not one of them, it seemed it would have been appropriate.

There's no escape. Other realities that bring us down can be dealt with, by denial or stupid bullheadedness. Low self-esteem is permeable to cons and shyster tricks. If you think you're too short, get special shoes or dress tall. If you're not smart, do what I did when I was twelve and resolve to be sexy to compensate. (I'm still working on it, but I suspect it's a lost cause.) But not aging. Nothing works.

In a restaurant I won't name, in an anonymous city, with two friends whose names I will also have the courtesy to leave out of this brief narrative, I spent a few hours last year, in the lair of the lotophagi—the lotus eaters (a mythical race of people whose principal diet of lotus fruits and flowers was addictive and engendered sleep and apathy). It was a swell restaurant, with large, comfortable booths, and bright (too bright) lights. The men wandered between booths, meeting and greeting friends, all bright Pepsodented and perfected teeth and frightened eyes, draped in silks and tailored wool, with fat gold nugget watches and diamond rings. The women sat nearly motionless in the booths in their designer finery and rare jewels, not smiling. Not smiling, I suspect, because they couldn't: all around me were examples of plastic surgery as craving endlessly and addictively fulfilled. They had lips and cheekbones and seamless foreheads above wide-open eyes that went beyond mere vanity and into the distorted vision of cartoons or drawings by George Grosz. It was sad to see—the women perched in their booths, and the men fluttering about the room, in constant flight from even a moment of repose.

The steaks were fork-tender and thick, the green beans were surreal in their bright green enormity, and the baked potatoes perfect. I was gulping down the food, heedless of appetite, bent low over the outsized china, trying, I now believe, to dull my overworked senses. My friends had seen it, too, this Grand Guignol scene, and we ate in silence. Finally, around a mouthful of dripping blood-rare steak, I whispered, "Thank God I've stopped doing acid."

It was pitiful and sad, and they seemed such victims, these lotus eaters.

Says me.

Since I turned sixty, I have gotten six tattoos, bought and sold a Harley, learned to surf, dated a woman twenty-five years my junior, grown my hair almost to my shoulders, shaved my head, fantasized about things that are none of your business, and done some of them. I really thought that I was exempt. If you're an addict, I suspect you can understand that feeling. When I first stopped drinking and using, I was at least a little astonished that somehow I, the golden child, had "become" an alcoholic and even felt, for a while, that I could just take a little break and then go back to all the fun I'd been having.

I was *puer aeternus,* the boy child who would never age, Peter Pan in search of the next adventure or even, maybe, a

Wendy who would take care of me, just like mommy did, while I continued in my boyish ways, heedless of time and reckless.

When I finally admitted I was an alcoholic, I was chagrined. However, when I finally saw I was old, I was greatly relieved: That explained it! I was already secretly grateful, for example, for the diminished libido, as was Sophocles who spoke of the great relief of that loss. Ever grandiose, however, I quickly aligned myself with my ancient Taoist heroes who gave up sex (and grains, for some reason) when they reached their later years. I am quite skillful at making a virtue of necessity. So let me be clear, being old is no virtue. Nor is it a mistake, a momentary inconvenience, or, as my good friend and kind physician Bruce Branin pointed out to me on the day that we found that my formerly passive blood pressure was in the danger zone, a sign of me being "wrong." I was old. Early old, but old.

Members of Alcoholics Anonymous are cautioned early on that it is vital to "let go of our old ideas" in order to enter into that great promise of the Twelve Step programs, "the joy of living." Over the years it has become clear to me that my old ideas are often the ideas I had yesterday.

Emily Dickinson spoke of "slant truth," which, to my mind, means truth from a different perspective. What happened in my life on July 16, my oblivion reverie, needed to be seen from a different perspective. It is my belief that one of the gifts of growing older is the ability, perhaps even the dogged insistence, to turn the truth at an angle and peer at it, ever open-minded, to see where the real truth is and to dismiss what it has seemed to be in the past. Thinking about a drink was a great gift. It was not a mere symptom, nor was it, I will insist, dangerous or somehow a sign that I was doing something "wrong." My psyche was facing something it had never faced before and returned, reluctantly, to the old ideas. Getting old? Don't want to? Get drunk! Or act out in other grotesque ways, of course, like buying a motorcycle or getting tattoos or, not for me but always there, the god Botox. Surrender unto the plastic surgeon the things of the lesser gods! Worship Viagra (and risk going blind)! Learn to surf!

What is the "slant truth" of being old? I think we've made the first step, don't you? I'm powerless over age, and my life was becoming silly. So it's time to find power once more, the subject of the pages right ahead.

*"Without my journey*
*And without the spring*
*I would have missed this dawn."*
—Masaoka Shiki (1867–1902)

## Two Truths

My elder years have now become the time to let go of what I've been taught and to remember what I've always known.

It is my time, entirely, the time that the masks come off and all the wandering leads home.

My days are precious now, and to squander them would be to squander my life. If I miss the dawn, I miss an opportunity to live fully through the day, content within its rhythms and darkness.

I get up long before dawn these days. It's a useful habit I've learned through writing five books and that I first learned as a Tennessee farm boy. Back then I milked cows.

I was busy. Now the cows are gone, but there are plenty of chores to do. Too many, I think. These days, I have added something to these early hours and—more pointedly—I have taken a lot away. What I don't do is this: No e-mail, no television, no *New York Times,* and I even practice a little discipline with caffeine. The cigars are still with me, on occasion. What I do is this: I put some medicinal herbs in a pot to soak for an hour. I go into the living room, which is practically empty of furniture but for six small, round black cushions on top of six large, rectangular black cushions, and a Japanese tea table with an iron teapot and two iron cups. I set the meditation timer for an hour and fold myself onto the cushions I've been using for many years now.

I sit for the full hour as the sky lightens. The herbs soak. I soak. One particular morning, not long ago, the living room was streaked with moonlight, brighter than usual, it seemed, and then the sweet light of day arose. It was dawn and all was well.

When the gong rings, I bow and mutter a phrase or two of some teachings of a loving kindness prayer, and I often speak aloud the prayer of St. Francis, paying particular attention to the phrase "it is in self forgetting that one is found." I read whatever poetry I feel like reading. I often speak directly with God. (More about that later.) This is a kind of Christian/Buddhist/eclectic meditation, with no home but my own. I unfold, creaking and muttering phrases that are less loving and less kind, and go into the kitchen, where I have some coffee and set the herbs to simmer. That takes a while. The herbs simmer. I simmer. During that time I write a letter to my son, something I've done daily for four years.

My morning schedule on yet another ordinary Monday morning in early March of 2008 was no different than any other recent one, and yet it was entirely different.

I had been having a very hard time writing this book. I'd been stuck, drowning, gasping for clean air. I had a huge stack of books, manila folders full of magazine and news-paper articles, as well as many additional articles and papers I'd pulled off the Internet. I had source material that is thousands of years old, other material from the forties and fifties of the last century, and some that is as new as yester-day. I was buried in other people's words.

Now then: Whenever I meditate, I continually dismiss thoughts, gently, as they arise. Eventually, the thoughts or, more often, images, become far apart, but the ones that arise then are cooked down and insistent and, I believe, very good for unclogging my spiritual and emotional arteries. After a while, on that turning morning, all that I could see, in my mind's eye, was that stack of books and manila folders surrounding me. "Interesting," I thought, and then I let it go and returned to my breath. Time passed. Then, I swear, something that looked like a bumper sticker arose from a deep place. I followed it. In brilliant blue script on a white background, it said, "Keep It Simple." I shouted "aha!" It was loud and joyous. My cat, Fred, who was sitting on the larger cushion as usual, leapt up, ready, once more, to confront those damned cocker spaniels from down the block.

I'd been trying to write someone else's book. All I can really do, I realized, is tell my story, as simply as possible. So this turned into the most personal book I've ever written, when I had thought it had to be the "smartest" and most complex. Underneath all the reading, the intellectual curiosity, I'm really quite simple, and I discovered that "smart," meaning scholarly, just isn't me. Once I remembered that, I hoped I could follow the example of the great poets and reduce what I had to say to a few words, and the right ones. Eventually, I realized I couldn't—the forms don't mix. So finally, I endeavored to just stand out of the way and point to what is on the other side of the door of my mind, rather than standing in the doorway, blocking the view and merely describing what's there, glancing over my intrusive shoulder occasionally.

At my age, there is little left to do but to stop moving so much, breathe, let go, pay attention, carve away the unessential, help everyone who wants to be helped—and tell the truth.

This book began with a frightening look I had, unbidden, at my vulnerability as I age, my spooky denial that

I was aging at all, and how, faced with something hitherto unknown, the suffering of aging, I moved to my most familiar medicines—Jack Daniel's whiskey, Camel cigarettes, and splendid isolation.

That singular moment made it clear to me that what I had learned as a much younger man, using only the steps of Alcoholics Anonymous as my spiritual practice, was out of date and wasn't enough now. I saw, in quite infrequent glimpses of insight, that I needed to "re-vision" my life and reinvent the meaning of "sobriety" in order to fit this new mind and new body so that I could continue to experience the unfolding enlightenment that began on that somber night of whiskey, cigarettes, and welcome distance from the whole of the world I had known for twenty-three years.

I also saw that my life is multidimensional and that every event of my life can be viewed from different angles, with different shards of light illuminating a whole life full of discrete moments. When I was alone on my horse as a child, galloping, standing up in the stirrups, was I isolating, running from my maternal grandmother, or was I acting in response to a guardian angel that wanted me to experience the remarkable reality of being one with an enormous animal, in control while out of control, hell-bent at full speed across fallow cornfields?

For any one of those myriad moments, which presented themselves during this psychic cloak-and-dagger adventure, did I experience pathology or wholeness—or even a mythic life event? I saw that the choice was mine and that with the insight of my aging mind, I could reframe my life as ordinary or sacred. The true view is that it is both. Sacred and ordinary arise together, eternally locked in a gentle lover's embrace.

Looking back from the distance of age at events I had last looked at closely over twenty years before, revealed the sacred nature of every one of those events and more besides.

So an unexpected journey began as I sat, drunk, in my family room, and was made more vivid and personal as I sat, open and willing and honest, on a little black cushion, talking to God, several months later.

I saw that I have lived in two truths for my entire life, and that my addiction and my folly, once I quit drinking and using drugs, was deeply rooted in that contradiction. I don't think I'm alone in that folly. Only through the process of "bitter searching of the heart," as Leonard Cohen murmurs it, did I reconcile the opposites and go on "to play a greater part."

The contradiction? Quite simple, once I saw it, but I believe it took the breadth of my years to do so. My central and largely unacknowledged dilemma has been that I have lived two truths.

I lived in the world of consensus reality, which was a world of power, and I lived in an inner world, based in the senses, which was a world of love. The Lover, within, suffered for many years.

But I could not have known that when I began this inquiry.

I needed to know my story, anew. And then I needed to let it go and simply be still. After story there is only silence, only the whispered words of God.

It is in the deep silence, below story, in stillness and the barest of attention, that I can hear the voice of God. In that stillness, not so long ago, an unexpected vision arose, prophetic and mysterious and with facets I have yet to explore. This book ends with it.

*"[The self-centered one] is like the
retired business man who lolls in
the Florida sunshine in the winter
complaining of the sad state of the nation."*
**Alcoholics Anonymous, 4th Edition (page 61)**

# The Downward Slope

The words above were written in 1939, probably by AA
cofounder Bill Wilson.

Whoever penned them is my spiritual ancestor. These
words are just snarly enough to fit into my lexicon and are
dead-on accurate in describing the cliché of "retirement."

I will not "retire." To what?

I am not a "senior citizen."

I am not much of a citizen at all if *citizen* means that I
follow the rules and do what is expected of one of these
"senior citizens." That's a term that is supposed to confer
honor, and we know that it is just the opposite. It is our
culture's way of saying: "Cut 'em out of the herd and let

'em wander. I know—we'll open the shopping malls early so they can do their cute walking and look in the windows of all the closed shops at the things they can't buy any longer. Trust me—they'll like that."

Everyone ages. Not everyone who ages is old, however. And there's the pity of it all. I can imagine that there are readers who read that sentence and thought, "Aha, this guy's got it! You're only as old as you think you are." That's true. What else is true is that to be old is a very good thing. Aging is not all there is to being old. I know a young man of eighteen who many say has an "old soul." So—what is old?

"I intend to enjoy my life on the downward slope." The head of a convent in a northern state, who shall remain anonymous, said those words to me.

I was at the convent conducting a three-day seminar on addiction. The crowd was larger than expected, and I was a touch nervous. This particular monastic, fully garbed in a modified wimple and veil, came to me backstage and asked if there was anything she could do. She had noticed I seemed nervous. Without thinking, I said, "A little heroin would be nice." She giggled—really, she giggled—and said that she reckoned if she had any she'd keep it for herself. I was relaxed at once. There is great power in humor, even the self-deprecating type, if used cautiously. She and I went on to talk about the depth of the winter. I asked how the residents handled the harsh weather. "There are only three of us left now. This world is fading out, but so am I." Another giggle.

I stayed away from any false comfort and asked if she was going to be there for the rest of her life or if retirement was part of the package for a mother superior. She told me she was through, but would probably stay at the monastery, because of the comfort there. And it was then that she said she intended to enjoy life "on the downward slope." I've used the term ever since, and I'm grateful to her for it.

One more bit of gratitude, and then we'll move on (or down). Just as I was being introduced to the folks waiting in the auditorium, she asked if I was still nervous. I allowed as to how I was. "Take off your boots and walk out there in your socks and tell them about it!" she commanded. I did. I actually did the entire three days of formal retreat barefoot. You have no idea how liberating that can be!

If you're like me, everything that used to go up is starting to go down. We grow "up" for years; we are on the "upward" track in our careers, our social lives. We firm "up;" we keep our chins "up;" we even throw our hands "up." And, of course, we throw up in general when we're having too much fun. Upward and outward we go for years. And then it ends. A friend who is now in his seventies told me that one morning, when he was sixty-five, he woke up ("up" of course, we don't wake "down") and found that he was old. His first thought was, "I really am going to die." And then they put us down in the ground, one way or another. In the grave. So getting old is a "grave" business, the yawning reality at the end of the downward slope, almost never seen unless we make the jump consciously.

There is a dangerous assumption in what I've just written. By mocking physiology, I am saying that physiology alone governs aging. All of the research that I have read on aging seems directed toward one aim—to put an end to aging, as if it were tuberculosis or AIDS, something that kills, but something we can overcome. "We shall overcome," creak the throats at the shopping mall doors, a long way from that other mall where many of my generation gathered decades ago.

If we are fortunate enough to have gotten old—the way my grandfather's rocking chair in which I am sitting writing these words has gotten old, the way my pocketknife, which fits my hand with such intimacy after thirty years, has gotten old—then we are the avatars, and our message is an important one: We are those who, each in our own way, led by our own daemons—those mythic creatures that seek to embody our personal destiny—have moved from the self-centered isolation of infancy and, for some of us, addiction, into the reality of *other*-centered intimacy. Otherness.

My friend Lenny is other than me, and we have great intimacy. But at a further remove and in ways that I am just beginning to understand, a dolphin in the Golfo Dulce of Costa Rica and a towering redwood in the coastal forests of Oregon are also other and are also included in this other-centered intimacy.

*Old,* in the best sense of the word, is synonymous with *dignity,* the dignity that comes from having moved from the complexity of growing up to the simplicity of growing down. There is a live oak tree in a cypress swamp near here that is hundreds of years old. It is often described as dignified. Lightning, erosion, hurricanes have not undermined or killed it. That thing is *tree,* my friend.

*"People like you and I,*
*though mortal of course like everyone else,*
*do not grow old no matter how long we live. . . .*
*[We] never cease to stand like curious children*
*before the great mystery into which we were born."*
—Albert Einstein
in a letter to Otto Juliusburger

# Old Is Good

"You're not wrong for growing old."

My doctor and dear friend, Bruce Branin, said that to me when I was sixty-four and we discovered that my blood pressure was not within safe limits. It was bad enough that I needed trifocals and had only three of the teeth left that I had so carefully grown during my early years. My hearing was going, my hair was, I prefer to say, silver (read gray), and as the poet says, I ached in the places where I used to play. But high blood pressure?

Old people have high blood pressure.

I'm going to give away right now what is the over-riding prejudice of this book. I suppose I should save it for the end, but planning for the future is not something I do much anymore. So here is the prejudice.

Old is good.

That's a choice, not a universal reality. It is also my experience, thus far, although I am admittedly still young relative to where my family history says I'll go.

For one thing, I have done it: I've gotten old. My young friends haven't done that yet. I survived multiple hospitalizations for having a few too many cocktails; I went through a difficult divorce without killing anyone; I have watched friends die, as well as both of my parents. I did enough psychedelics to turn on my old Haight-Ashbury neighborhood for a day or two, and I drank and smoked cigarettes as if to do so was a mandate. I ate red meat and thought of vegetables as something for animals far lower in the food chain. I was a runner until my knees gave out. And yet, I've gotten older without caving in completely.

One myth is that with age comes wisdom. I'm not certain that I've gotten any wiser, but one gift of age is that I don't really mind.

Old is good. I am one of the fortunate ones in that I have finally managed to live my life, not someone else's. I reframed my life, with the vision and distance of age, and that has made all the difference. That is the process which informs much of this book. You can do it as well. All that is necessary is that you let go, absolutely, of all of your "old" ideas. You can read that either way you wish. Both are accurate.

But on the day that Bruce Branin told me that I had high blood pressure and that I wasn't wrong for growing old, my first thought was this: "Shit, I really am going to die." Nothing was good about old at that moment.

I'm going to die.

So are you. So is everyone, but this was *me* who had moved further up on the conveyor belt to the dustbin.

My mother lived a long life, rich with stories, and I'm going to tell you one here. She died at ninety-two. She was not well for many years prior to that, and the death of my father, her husband of sixty-five years, did her in. Her saddest cry during the five years she lay dying was, "I'm lonesome." This was a kind of existential aloneness, made more vivid by the death of her husband and so many of her friends, but I believe she touched the core of our ache.

Three days before she died, I was sitting by her bedside. She rarely got out of bed. There was a portable toilet just a shuffle away, and she had twenty-four-hour nursing care. The television was often on, but I don't think she really saw it. There was only the vast lonesomeness that penetrated her every moment. On that afternoon, three days before death would make its silent entry into her waning life, she looked at me through rheumy eyes and asked, "Billy, am I dying?" I told her she was, that we all are, but that she was at the head of the line.

"Thank God," she whispered.

There was a pause. Then, "Will I go to heaven?"

"Yes, Mom." It wasn't for me to interfere with her beliefs.

"Will I have my own star?"

"Yes, Mom, you will."

"Will your father be there?"

"Yes," again.

"Will he have his own star?"

"Yes."

Long pause.

"Will we fight?"

"No, Mom, all the fighting is over, all of it."

Again, "Thank God."

She died, alone, three days later. The nurse found her, called hospice, and then called me. Her memorial service was a good one, but sparsely attended. My brother and I both spoke. We interred her ashes in a wall, in the same crypt as my father's. Their stars.

We're lonesome, you and I, and we'd rather not face that truth. We die.

Here is my wish for you: that all the fighting be over, all of it, long before you die. I plan to go gentle into that good night. I will not rage against the dying of the light. To the contrary, I am becoming a creature of the dark. I thrive in moonlight, the light of potential and arising.

Sickness and aloneness are inevitable.

And still: Old is good.

That's a choice.

Our conditioning of a lifetime comes to bear on those days of aging. We fear it. Fear is aggression toward self. "I'm aging and I am afraid" becomes a subtle hatred.

This hatred is reinforced by a culture that fears age, that sees age as a mistake, a failure of will, a form of punishment for not eating our vegetables and hiding our money under the mattress, where we are rendered ugly and useless or, at best, useful only for petty tasks. Or we are useful, you and I, as we age, to prove that, in fact, aging is a mistake, a cosmic error that can be overcome, so we are encouraged to take up marathon running or to follow silly old Dennis Hopper into materialistic fantasies of houses in the desert or into dreams of doing all those things that young people do.

I am old. I do not do what young people do. I do what I do. I am not falling into decrepitude; I am rising to play a greater and different part. I creak when I rise.

The fear, the hatred, the self-aggression is reinforced by the culture, and it is the culture that has conditioned us from the very start. The conditioning is ancient. Jesus spoke against it, as did Isaiah and the Buddha and Lao-tzu. Kurt Vonnegut, too, and Mark Twain. The wise ones got that way by breaking the chains of conditioning, not by pulling 'em tight and clicking the locks closed.

Here is the lifelong curse, deepened and weathered by aging:

"I should," with its vicious echo, "I should not."

It is a default for so many of us and a sure predictor for addiction, that desperate clinging to anything that helps us avoid facing our fear of not fitting in, of being forgotten.

There is another, deeper prejudice, one that you and I carry that makes the lure of addiction more vivid, more promising.

We believe that the elders are discarded, that it is our fate to be on the margins for up to one-third of our life. It is a sad truth that fully one-third of our elder population is living in poverty or are so poor that they cannot afford necessary medications and healthy food. Of the million or so living in what are euphemistically called "nursing homes," the majority are living lives of deprivation, with no nursing going on at all. You and I hear these stories and are touched with a frisson of dread that says, "That's going to be me."

During a period I am not proud of, in the late sixties, I worked as a "chase man" for a loan company. It was my distasteful job to hunt down people who had defaulted on loans that were usurious in the first place. There was one fellow who frightened me more than any other. He was in his sixties and lived in a squalid room in a single-room occupancy hotel near the rail yards in San Francisco. He smelled of urine and cigarette smoke. His floor was littered with tall Budweiser cans. He didn't eat anything but sardines and crackers, and he had the gray pallor of one near death. I saw him, we talked, and I walked away as if I had never found him. Neither of the options that I could think of were good ones. I could not bear to turn him in, but, worse, I could not imagine going back to see him.

In my worst moments, drunk or sober, that man is the ghost who haunts me, who activates and personifies my deepest fears. I don't fear death. I am making my peace with aging and with sickness. But I am dazed and made hopeless by the fear of being ignored, in that very SRO room, with the sounds of the gray San Francisco rail yard penetrating my welcome stupor, overwhelming even my death stench.

We are not separate from those who are aging in suffering, those who are discarded by a culture that does not want to be reminded of the reality of sickness, old age, and death.

We buy the images of the culture, those of youth and beauty, as marketable skills (how foolish, to see an accident as a skill), and we feel the fears of becoming the Discarded Ones.

> *"So our troubles, we think, are basically*
> *of our own making. They arise out of ourselves,*
> *and the alcoholic is an extreme example of*
> *self-will run riot, though he usually doesn't think so."*
> —*Alcoholics Anonymous*, 4th Edition (page 62)

## We Are Addicts

If our fears of being discarded and forgotten are not acknowledged and embraced, the end result is all but predictable.

Addiction.

I think I've had enough of that and suspect that since you're reading this book, you have as well. I'm hardwired for the gross addictions: alcohol, sex, nicotine, narcotics, psychedelics, and amphetamines.

But we are a nation, a culture, of addicts. I am sure you realize by now that this book is for anyone who might think their life is out of balance, with the bar tilting toward darkness and despair and addiction. You don't have to have drunk the Pacific Ocean or snorted most of Bolivia to be in that situation.

We're addicts. If we aren't addicted to drugs and alcohol, perhaps it's to work or sex or service or, the most pernicious, "self-improvement." There it is, you see.

The ultimate addiction is the addiction to the perfected self. My former Zen teacher once asked me, "What makes you so special? Show me anyone who is not addicted."

In many parts of the world, *lazy* is a word for a kind of somnolence, a *mañana* attitude that I find quite compelling. I've lived in the tropics, and the torpor was luscious. The heat stirred up creative energy. But, no, the mainland, twenty-first century, first-world laziness is of a different type.

Here is its most insipid and pernicious symptom: multitasking. What more effective way to avoid the truth than by becoming what Benjamin Hoff calls "Bisy Backson," (a term taken from A. A. Milne's *Winnie the Pooh*). Here he is. Do you recognize him?

> Backson thinks of progress in terms of fighting and overcoming. One of his little idiosyncrasies, you might say. Of course real progress involves growing and developing, which involves changing inside, but that's something the inflexible Backson is unwilling to do. (*The Tao of Pooh*)

In our so-called productive years, we rush out of bed in the morning, often awakened by "alarm" clocks. What an awful way to start the day, in a state of alarm! "Dammit, I've got to get going, the alarms are going off!"

Taking a shower, we wonder about having time to eat. Eating a packaged food product, packed with vitamins and minerals and, probably, fiber and EFAs—whatever those are—we wonder if there's enough gas in the car so we can get to work "on time." An hour into the day, and we've been alarmed, rushed, force-fed, and stuffed into a machine to get somewhere where we can produce something.

Sounds like a feedlot to me. All that's lacking is standing in our own waste products. (I did that a few times when I was drinking, and that was enough.)

It's not over.

Throughout the day, we coddle the delusion of busyness and planning. In our days as employees we did so, and is it that different now? We live lives of constant distraction, most of it sought in our headlong flight from reality. There are millions of diversions, sought and unsought. The football game, the charity work, the volunteering, the civic duties dutifully performed. Are these somehow "wrong"? No, not in balance, but it is the lifelong lack of balance that becomes infinitely grave as we grow older. And the social life. I go dancing every week and members of that community are becoming friends over time, in spite of their aggressive youth, in many cases. I bicycle, I study a martial art, and, being without regular employment, I can do all that and more on my own schedule and with greater flexibility.

So how is this laziness?

Thich Nhat Hanh, another of my teachers, speaks of missing our appointment with life.

We all learned in schools that Socrates found that "the unexamined life is not worth living."

In all our busyness, we never look in the mirror; we never see who we really are.

I spoke, earlier, of my dispiriting experience at a restaurant, surrounded by old people who looked like they fed on the young. They do. They absorb the contaminated shadow of lifeblood with their toxins, their chemical peels, their face-lifts, their bloody beef and cool gin.

This is denial and excess to the point of living the life of a classical tragic clown, unable to dance, face frozen in a rictus mask, posing in the court of a dark king.

William Blake said that "the road of excess leads to the palace of wisdom."

That statement has become a cliché and I, for one, used it to justify my behavior for many years. My excesses were all of the "material" type—partying, hitchhiking cross-country, drinking epically, being a wild man in a way that was really stupefying and practiced—a poseur, if you will.

Such excess really needs to have an internal prod, a kind

of existential rawness that summons dragons and tigers to roam the landscape, internal and external.

In our younger years, the excess can be compulsive scheduling and working and consuming. We become the Hungry Ghost of Tibetan iconography (a creature with a vast body and a skinny neck who can never, ever get enough, even in such an abundant world as that which it inhabits).

Such excess, such endless longing and addiction, is another mask. Beneath it is the face of the lost one, life out of balance, who wants only to end its suffering.

I finally got to the real point of it, or so I thought. I quit drinking, gave up excessive ambition, and embarked—more consciously, but still lost—on what I saw as a spiritual path. Then the "excess" became a kind of spiritual and intellectual inquiry that was without boundaries or much discipline. This was a good thing, but I may have carried it on for too long. The road of excess does in fact lead to the palace of wisdom, but it's useful to recognize the palace when you've gotten there and to step off the road. There, in a long moment of holistic awareness, the depth of the spiritual life is revealed. The spiritual life is said to be marked by chaos, then obedience, then skepticism, and, finally, integration into "the undifferentiated," that is, the place of loving acceptance of reality or arrival at the palace, and seeing that it contains absolutely everything in its vast emptiness.

Most religious scholars seem to feel that, in this culture

at least, we never get past the second stage, obedience, which explains the prevalence of fundamentalism.

I learn more from the existential awareness of Wendy and Henry and Jim and Chris and Naomi and Gracie and the whole mad crowd of people in my life than I will ever learn from some dead book. But the book, all the books, and the rules, all the rules, offer certainty and meaning in a world that, to the fearful mind, offers none.

What have I taken from all this?

First, read the books. They are important. And learn the rules. They are important. Then put the books and the rules away and live in the questions, right here and right now. Then, if you've really dropped the books and sensed the way things are, live in the Palace of Wisdom—a shelter where generosity and joy abound.

A place of balance.

> *"We do not grow absolutely, chronologically. We grow sometimes in one dimension, and not in another; unevenly. We grow partially. We are relative. We are mature in one realm, childish in another. The past, present, and future mingle and pull us backward, forward, or fix us in the present. We are made up of layers, cells, constellations."*
>
> —Anaïs Nin

# The God of Time

In Twelve Step programs, we hear of the demons of irritability, restlessness, and discontent, and the Buddha spoke of "suffering" as a chronic sense of unsatisfactoriness, anxiety, disturbance, irritation, dejection, worry, despair, and fear. In Matthew, Jesus says, "Come unto me, all ye that are weary and heavy laden, and I will give you rest."

An old friend, looking at these realities, once said to me while sitting in a coffee shop in late afternoon in the SoHo section of New York City, "Birth, sickness, old age, and death. What a curriculum!"

As I discovered that night when I went on a mind search for oblivion, lost in a fantasy of whiskey and cigarettes, the curriculum never changes. Over the years, I had become skilled in the use of my eclectic spiritual practice in order to face the reality of suffering and the reality, or truth, of release from suffering. But I was, and I still am, only part of the way through the curriculum. Confident in my shallow understanding, I had rested between classes.

This is the point of the coming of age and, with it, a new set of challenges, but without a rule book. There is no default for this one, and the risks are heavy, the punishments severe.

On that night of the fantasy escape into oblivion, Chronos beckoned. In Greek mythology, Chronos is the god of time, usually depicted as a wise and decrepit old man. In my private mythology, he is the bringer of age, and it is he who stands in front of Thanatos, the god of death, revealing him only in glimpses.

That night, I returned to my default solution, if only in my mind.

Addiction. The welcome and stealthy death, wrapped in a golden cloak.

In the fall of 2004, I had my first experience of being consciously touched by Chronos. I didn't recognize it, at first, this gentle nudge. I had lived for several weeks with a sense of doom and uncertainty. There was nothing special going on in my life to bring this about. I awoke every morning with a sense of profound disinterest in the day to come. The days trudged along, and I followed. Something was sadly out of balance. I called a friend on the West Coast and told her about it, and she made a remarkable suggestion. First off, she told me that my problem was that I was getting old. Well, I was only sixty-two at the time, so I dismissed that foolish idea out of hand. She went on to say that I should sit in meditation and, uncharacteristically for the rather severe form of meditation we practiced, listen to music. More specifically, she told me to listen to the fifth movement of Holst's symphony *The Planets.* That is "Saturn: The Bringer of Old Age."

I didn't, of course.

If she had said that all I had to do each day was light a stick of incense and shout the word *mu* and my day, and life, would be perfect and fully realized, I wouldn't have done that, either. Such is my defiance.

Instead, I sat down in meditative posture and listened to the seventh movement, "Neptune: The Mystic." After all, I had read Evelyn Underhill's book on the subject, and I was aware of the flowing together of the Via Dolorosa (the "way of suffering," a route in Jerusalem traditionally thought to be the path that Jesus walked to his crucifixion) and the Ten Ox-Herding Pictures from the Zen tradition, which depict the road to awakening, ending with the awakened one entering the marketplace with bliss-bestowing hands. That was me, certainly. And I knew, with unruly faith, that it was Neptune who would speak to me.

Wrong.

The days passed like sludge. Nothing was better. It was hurricane season, and a bad one for Florida. The air was heavy, the skies often threatening.

On the September day that Hurricane Frances hit, I was at the lowest of ebbs. Like the weather, I was torpid and dense, rich with danger.

I finally put on "Saturn," set it on repeat, folded myself into the meditation posture on my glassed-in back porch, overlooking live oak trees, their wraithlike festoons of Spanish moss whipping in the waxing wind, and I sat and let the storm and the music inhabit me.

Frances was a bad hurricane. It was a small miracle that the cacophony didn't break me out of the music and another that my electricity didn't go out. The trees moved and one old oak finally cracked with the dying shriek of a banshee and fell, missing my house by only a few yards. The winds yowled in the trees and spoke in unmusical whispers under the eaves of my house.

"Saturn" played on. Its tones are deliberate and rich. The tempo is that of movement that is not meant to surprise, but to gently warn of "something happening here." There is a sense of a great being, a saint, a god perhaps, coming over the horizon, slow and steadfast, unstoppable and sure in its progress. The legs, then the trunk, then the aged face appear, in sequence, as the clouds lift, from earth to heaven.

In the midst of the storm, I felt the presence of potential, of what I didn't know, and of calm. There was a matrix, for the moment, of possibility and safety. I listened to the music over and over, as the storm waxed and waned. I got the message, beneath full consciousness, that my friend the Zen master wanted me to get. It was mine alone, of course, filtered through sixty-two years of living experience, but the master knew me. It helped that she is my age.

"I'm getting old. Damn. Even me." I had entered a new phase, a beginner again.

I think I am like the legendary mule that is so stubborn that the farmer must hit him in the forehead, full force, with a two-by-four, just to get his attention.

I am not much for the mystic "sciences," such as astrology, but I find that one, in particular, is a useful background for understanding my larger mind.

Saturn, I found, is the planet that ushers in the possibility of wisdom, particularly in later years. OK. In conversation with my friend John Marchasella, an astrologer, I also found that Saturn is the planet—or, in my preference, the god—of settling accounts.

Saturn brings age and a chance to set the ledger straight before moving on. (In the symphony, the next planets are Uranus: The Magician, and Neptune: The Mystic. We shall see.)

I was at a crossroads. It would take three more years for the signs to become visible, but a journey I couldn't have packed my luggage for was about to begin.

If I paid attention, I know now, I would be offered the

opportunity to turn my back on chaos and authority and enter, for the final time, the valley of skepticism.

So, we are at a point of crisis. This is the sacred catastrophe. For those of us with addictions to the grosser substances, this seems to be nothing new. But it is entirely new.

This is a catastrophe of spirit, mind, and body that we have not caused or prepared for. "I'm an addict" can be fixed. "I'm old" can't.

So what do we do? What is the first step here?

The first step is to spend some time in meditation on this reality: There is no linear progression, fixed in time and space, in which all the many aspects of our human life— no matter our age—grow or change at the same rate. We approach, we move back, we grow, we stagnate, we regress. The mechanism is changing, but the spirit, the mind, the soul, the so-called maturing, is chaotic. We demand certainty, but by now, you and I have hopefully learned that we ain't gonna get it.

We are learning about the chaos, the uncertainty, and the explosive/implosive nature of our aging.

Dancing on the edge of life and death, we are responsible, we are powerful, we are free.

Those of us who have moved out of our grosser addictions know there is another option—to be of service. Elsewhere, I have written about moving past the zero of balanced atonement. In that case, I have made amends to those I have hurt, and all is in both balance and stasis. To move past zero is to serve those whom I might have become. It's easily done for those in Twelve Step programs; too easily, I fear.

I serve my peers. My choice is to determine who those peers are. As I have moved from a self-centered life to an other-centered life, it has become clear who they are. Everyone.

Who is excluded?

In 1985, I was walking on Madison Avenue in New York City with my good friend (and, I see now, elder sage) Lou. We passed a church right next door to the glitzy home base store of Ralph Lauren, he who purveys the fantasy of "old money" at high new-money prices. On the steps of the church, there was a sad group of homeless people, waiting to be fed. There were pint bottles and cigarette butts in evidence.

As we passed, I said to my friend, "There, but for the grace of God, go I." Lou stopped dead still, grabbed my arm, turned me to face him, and said, almost in anger, "No, hotshot, you've got it wrong. It's 'There go I.'"

On these pages, I will say to you, "Ah, there go I." When you see the homeless ones, the beaten ones, the drunken and addicted ones, and, yes, even the powerful and rich and suffering ones, you can say, as an elder, "There go I."

And you'll be right!

*"I don't want to achieve immortality through my work . . .*
*I want to achieve immortality by not dying."*
—Woody Allen

# The End

The downward slope ends. Slowly or all at once, it ends. Then, perhaps, there is nothing, forever. Death comes when old age moves out. The body fails, often through the process of ischemia, from the Greek *ischaimos.* Blood is held and does not reach the places where it is needed. When our cells, our limbs, our hearts are not nourished, they diminish in their abilities, and they die.

Each death is different, marked by the life of the man or the woman whom it has come to. In death, as in birth, we are unique.

I could not in good conscience write this book about aging and leave out the inevitable end of that process; the inevitable end that is catholic and rooted solely in the reality that we are all of the nature to age and to die. Some of us just do the first of the two longer than others. Nonetheless, I hesitated to write about death. I'm so superstitious that I carried a hidden belief that if I talked about my death, then it would come, right away, midsentence, and carry me off in divine retribution for my heresy.

In reality, that would be no more than an ugly coincidence and—another reality—it is the only part of this aging process I am writing about for which I can claim no firsthand experience. So I looked at secondhand experience and a few teaching stories. Here's one.

My father took six years to die. He once told my brother, Philip, that he wouldn't wish the life he was living then on his worst enemy. Such was his humility. His wife of over sixty years, our mother, was with him every step of the way for all those years and, obdurately, was going to take care of him during this illness. She was in her late eighties, and caring for him was a terrible chore. For the last three years, he had in-home nursing care around the clock, but Mom was ever-present. The truth be told, she was often a problem to the nurses and even to Dad. She moved more slowly and often insisted on doing things the way she had learned in far-off, long-ago Mississippi, as a young girl.

Philip and I both spent as much time with our parents as we could during the end times for them; one of us came down to Florida at least once a month, alternating months. On one of those visits, watching Mom and her valiant efforts to help Dad, I decided to have a talk with her. I had been sober for double-digit years and had been a Zen student and practitioner for nearly as long. I sat down with Mom in the family room and we talked.

Actually, I talked. She listened. She was shrunken from osteoporosis and frail, with purple blotches on her hands and forearms from IVs administered during hospital visits for two small strokes, a broken wrist, and two joint replacements.

I talked. I delivered some speech full of "let go, let God," "care begins with self-care," "surrender," and on and on. Finally, I noticed that her eyes were glazed over—a bad sign. I stopped.

"Mom, do you have any questions?"

"Yes, Billy. I was wondering how much longer I was going to have to listen to this horseshit."

Not another second.

And then, her greatest teaching.

"You know, Billy, sometimes people just need to be held." Let's keep that in mind, OK?

Everybody's going through something, and it might be a good idea to learn to hold each other.

That day, I stood up, walked across the room, and held my mother. She cried.

Here's another teaching story.

The student asked the teacher, "What happens to us when we die?"

The teacher responded, "I don't know."

The student persisted. "What happens to us when we die?"

The teacher repeated, gently, "I don't know."

The student said, "But, you're supposed to know, you're a great master!"

The teacher said, "Yes, but not a dead one."

No one knows what it's like to die, as no one has survived the process. Sure, some have reported going a long way into it, of being clinically dead, but they ended up alive after all, and who knows what happens right after those reports of a celestial staircase or an infinite spiral or the trials of the in-between in Tibetan belief. Maybe right after that there is a big party at Giants Stadium, where all the enemies of the recently departed are buried up to their necks on the fifty-yard line and gleefully decapitated by ghouls who skip merrily amid the flying heads and spraying blood. Maybe. Or there really might be pearly gates with an angel who stands behind the rope, determining who is worthy of coming to the heavenly nightclub and who is not. Maybe.

We don't know, but we do know, as either observers or as central figures, that life includes illness and aging and, finally, death. And as clever, frightened, and narcissistic as I am, I would like to find a way to beat it. If only all those vitamin pills and Chinese herbs and all this daily exercise really did what I would like, I'd be like Methuselah—or even better, since he eventually died. Maybe heavy spiritual practice will do it! Or the Twelve Steps! Probably not. But they both can help break us out of the fear.

What about those Taoist immortals I read about? In philosophical Taoism, the great sages achieve enlightenment and never die. Or the Christian promise of life everlasting, what about that?

What we do know is that old age, sickness, and death are a reality we cannot avoid. These are the eternal afflictions, and yet they can be our greatest teachers.

I didn't want to write this chapter at first because I thought I could somehow set aging apart from death. I had lived a life of relative balance for many years, twenty at least. And then, life went subtly out of balance when I was confronted with my aging. One day I was in balance, the next day I was out of balance and death had moved a long way across the game board to block my view of all the moves left to make. I was in check.

Subsequent to my night of oblivion, and several months later, I had a very real, albeit brief, confrontation with my own death, moving one square closer on the board. My doctor opined that there was a chance I had cancer of the esophagus. As seems to be the common experience, he told me that we needed to do some serious tests right away! "Right away" meant over three weeks from that moment. I guess the message was that we were going to find out if I had cancer fairly soon, so that I shouldn't worry about dying before the tests.

Time passed, and after the initial panic, I sat in meditation with the fear and saw it evaporate, dust in the wind, and I came to a new understanding.

I had followed my own advice—often given, rarely practiced—by sitting meditation, and the sitting had its usual effect. Thoughts arise, thoughts fall away. Breath arises, breath falls away. "I" arose and simultaneously began the process of that "I" falling away. No difference between me and the Barred Owl across the creek, no difference between me and the creek itself, which sometimes runs full and other times is dry.

I am truly not separate from the realities of birth and death.

I am not wrong to be growing old, and I am not making a mistake by getting sick. Death, when it comes, is not a failure.

Once we see the inevitability of death, we want to control it. The simple seeing through to *nothing, forever,* can accelerate lives of uncertainty, denial, confusion, and fear.

When I get into conversations about death with those

friends who are willing to have such a talk, there remains in all of us a desire to control our death. It's not death we're afraid of, we say, it's dying. We talk about the choices and the preferences. This one wants to die in her sleep, that one quickly, that one in the presence of family and friends, peacefully. My sword teacher asked me how I wanted to die. Let me assure you that when you are facing a sword master who is holding a sword with a thirty-two-inch blade, a piercing tip, and razor-sharp edges, that is not a comforting question. "Do you mean now?" I wondered.

Hoping to forestall the inevitable death-by-nicks, so famed in sword practice, I said, without thinking, that I would like to die of a massive heart attack while surfing the longest left-breaking wave on the planet, which is near my longed-for home in Costa Rica, at age ninety-five or beyond.

I think I'll hold out for that one.

I believe that it is both dying and death that we fear. I don't like change of any kind and will go to any length to avoid it, but those two? Done deals, a long time ago. It's my nature to be sick, to grow old, and to die. I can go into it the same ways I can go into any change, kicking and screaming, or with genuine acceptance, at depth. The intellect is useless here, after its first writing out of the death sentence.

I have been a relentlessly negative, difficult, and opinionated person for much of my life. For decades, I was like the character Johnny, played by Marlon Brando, in the 1953 film *The Wild One,* who, when asked what he was rebelling against, answered, "Whadd'ya got?"

Indeed, whadd'ya got?

Rebelling against death is fruitless, of course. But there are more subtle ways of rebelling than simply saying, "No, won't do it, it's wrong and stupid, screw you."

One way to rebel is to determine how it should happen. This includes, of course, the choice of suicide. I choose not to pursue that topic, other than to repeat that I once considered suicide, quite seriously, and decided against it. On another occasion, decades ago, I witnessed an attempted suicide by someone I loved, using my gun. Those two moments, my consideration of suicide and my lover's attempt, have shown me what an ultimately selfish act it would be for me and can be for others. *Can be,* not *is.* I have no global opinion on the matter.

And what about spiritual practice in which we learn not to discriminate? Then, perhaps, we can ignore death! Nope. That's just another form, and a viral one, of discriminating. To think that nondiscrimination is a way to ignore reality is the spiritual equivalent of putting our hands over our ears and blabbering nonsense when someone is saying what we don't want to hear.

"You're gonna die, you're gonna die."

"Blah blah blah blah blah, can't hear you, can't hear you!"

In this moment, I am alive. In the next moment I might be dead. That is what's true.

Many of us come to spiritual practice when the suffering of seeing what we think is reality becomes too much for us. When I quit drinking and using drugs, I believe that my deeper self, what I often think of as my guardian angel, said to me, "You're dying and too quickly."

Jessamyn West said that the spiritual awakening that does not awaken us to love "has roused the sleeper in vain." There's the answer, in my experience, to the three essential questions we ask ourselves: (1) What is real? (2) Who am I? and (3) What is life all about?

We awakened to love, you see.

Only to discover we were going to get old, get sick, and drop dead eventually. That can trump love in, well, a heartbeat.

So now what?

Our temptation, and our folly, is to deny or ignore death. The Buddha said: "I am of the nature to die. There is no way to escape death. . . . My actions are my only true belongings. I cannot escape the consequences of my actions. My actions are the ground on which I stand."

And in the Bible, we read that we are known by the fruits of our labor.

And in the Tao Te Ching, that old dragon of the fruitful darkness, Lao-tzu, says to "do your work/and then let go. Such is heaven" (my version).

It is only my actions that matter; old age, sickness, and death will always have their way. I cannot truly believe that I will outlive death. This *self* is doomed. And so, knowing that, why is it so hard to let go of the desire for fame, riches, praise, comfort, safety, or some sort of immortality? How come we continue to believe, against all odds, that we are exempt?

> *"We coddle thousand-gold selves, but*
> *we're only guests: change soon takes*
> *our treasure. Why not naked burial?*
> People need to get beyond old ideas."
> — T'ao Ch'ien
> [emphasis added by author]

# Naked Burial

In the course of writing this book, I have been going through a time of self-examination with a very wise man, whom I trust completely and who sometimes irritates me to the edge of my endurance—which is only a foot or two away, in any case—and have found, as I seem to have to continually rediscover, that my greatest folly is the sense that I am separate, from you, from God, from death, from all the causes of suffering. Beneath all of my so-called character defects, there lurks this one primal and universal folly that spreads poison on my comings and goings, regularly.

Me, die?

Yes, even *this* "thousand-gold self" will die.

"Self," that deluded mongrel!

I also believe, based on long experience, that heaven and hell are right here, right now, in every moment, and that my residence in one or the other depends on my choices. All I need to do is let go—of everything. I've read that our results are nil until we let go, absolutely. My delusional, conditioned ideas must be allowed, themselves, to die. Just as T'ao Ch'ien said, 1,580 years ago as of this writing.

The first step, then, is that I must accept the inevitability of death in the very center of my being. This is radical acceptance. *Radical* means "rooted." So, rooted firmly in my spirit is the full knowledge of dying and death. How is that done, and where?

In silence. Silence is not enough, but it still is where we must start. It is a wholehearted inquiry, this one.

In silence, I can experience the reality of God as personal, without the folly of believing that God is a person. I learn, as did Meister Eckhardt, that the eye with which I see God is the eye with which God sees me. In silence, the great reality of life and death appears, in every breath. Arising, falling away. I choose this, close at hand and intimate, not that, separate and to one side.

I have become intimate, at least, with the folly of drinking and drugging. There was no "it." *I* drank, *I* used drugs, and *I* did all of that in a dim-witted response to suffering and the sense of a life eternally out of balance, a destiny of affliction and only affliction, as I was flawed and defective. I was born that way and I would die that way.

Lord have mercy! Such drama!

I courted chaos and, to my vast surprise, found the possibility of creativity and intimacy. In solving that central riddle of my life, I could see the solution to all suffering. The frightened self drank. The one fearful of death was the one who drank. I later learned that the drunkard and the fearful one had very positive lessons to teach me. I got the first one, right away. The wound inflicted by the drunkard was the very wound where God entered. So it is with this fear of death. A Buddhist master once said that he felt the Twelve Steps of Alcoholics Anonymous were a splendid spiritual teaching and that he would merely replace the word *God* with the word *love.* My fear wounds are portals through which love enters, so gently that I scarcely notice its passage.

And there is one action I take, a few more words I have begun to internalize. I have been doing this, nearly every evening, since a spiritual meltdown back in 2003, dark days when I seriously considered choosing death at my own hand and then realized, through a bit of reading, that my choice was life. And love.

I read First Corinthians, chapter 13, verse 13: "But now abide faith, hope, love, these three; but the greatest of these is love." In my Bible, there is a headline above that verse that says, "The Way of Love."

I loved drinking and drugging until they turned on me. I was so attached to the phantom of pleasure that I continued using drugs and alcohol long past the time of pleasure being possible. It was only through a time of despair and awakening that I was able to become radically sober, as I consider myself to be. Most of the time.

I was attached, by fear, to death. Fear is strong glue. This death fixation, which rules us, inhibits our actions and often makes us behave in ways contrary to our own best interests. Death, long before it puts us in checkmate, runs us. It affects our social, physical, and spiritual lives, making our lives small long before they end.

Despair and awakening are not necessary in order to let go of the attachment to death.

It is a choice. Do I practice death or do I practice life?

When we are free of the fear of death, death dies. In the prayer of St. Francis we are told that it is only by dying that we awaken to eternal life.

John Donne writes, "And death shall be no more; Death, thou shalt die!" This is the promise of the resurrection.

Then there's the Taoist hermit who chained himself to the tree because he decided it was time to die. When he awoke to the reality of his fears, the chains were gone and he became immortal.

My first teacher said, "Dancing on the edge of life and death, you are free!"

Right here, right now. All of it!

"Why not naked burial?" indeed. Free of fear, everything let go, no death, no birth, only this, right here, before your naked self, as your naked self, in this moment.

Coming to grips with death is a part of coming to grips with aging. All we have to do is let go, absolutely, of our old ideas. We can let go of our old fear-based, pathology-driven ideas. Only then can we awaken to love.

Remembering

# Story/Memory

The joy of letting go is the theme of mindful aging.

I have been working at letting go of everything I was taught and remembering everything I knew all along.

It's an arduous path. Aging is not for the timid, not if you embrace it rather than avoid it. Avoiding is easy—it's what we do best in this culture, isn't it?

This chapter is about story—and memory. It is by story that we learn, above all. It is story that heals: the stories we learn and remember about ourselves—the true ones—and the stories we tell and the stories we hear. We can theorize all we wish, and we can have great intellectual knowledge of, say, addiction, but if we don't have stories to tell and stories to hear, the knowledge is only a shadow of reality.

As I have aged, I have found that I spend more time in the past than previously. For the past several years, I have wandered corridors long forgotten and looked at the ancestral portraits in shadowed libraries; I have felt the touch and texture of things long gone such as a shoelace when it broke, again, and I was far out in the cotton fields, or walking to the barn after being thrown by my horse, age ten. I hear voices of minor characters like the drunken field hand who came to the farmhouse door and asked if he could "take the little boy into town, give him a taste of corn liquor." I taste again the holiday cookies I pilfered from the kitchen. I smell the chlorine in the pool where the girl who would become my wife and bear our daughter swam as I watched, and then jumped in, wearing only my basketball shorts.

My past is recalled by small events. I am surrounded by the madeleines of Proust—those sweet cakes tasted in *Remembrance of Things Past* that opened up for him a flood of sensations and memories—shape-shifting endlessly. This is a reflexive occurrence of the aging mind, whether I want it or not. The past presents itself to me, stirred by current events, and yet those events seem to be present only to take me back to the past, to relive, to remember, and, perhaps, to convert my understanding of this life, in order to move into the larger life, at one with God and other.

It's our choice, this business of meaning, after all. It is also such that most of the stories we tell ourselves are not, ultimately, true. We tend to change the scenes and collapse several stories into one, even cannibalize old stories to build a new one. This is a good thing. It's storytelling at its most creative. In this method of storytelling, we can see the movement in our lives from egocentric to other-centric to eco-centric to, finally (if we're awake), cosmos-centric.

The mystery of childhood revisited and seen in new ways has taught me that I can look at my life in a way that is free of pathology and, better, a way that frees me from the endless murmuring of the injured self. I had for some time become invested in the story of woundedness, but its dividends were soon seen as meager.

It is also true that these traumas, even viewed from this new point of view, were real. When my mother humiliated me in front of the family, it was a wound that went deep. But now I am able to see how the wound contained the gift of revealing my destiny.

We live in a culture of woundedness. Daily talk shows bring us stories of wounds and anger. The so-called news programs cover the sordid shenanigans of the rich and famous who are addicted and in chaos, and the relentless coverage of their sad lives is the platform from which the media can tell us of the disease of the week and suggest that we ask our doctors for the drugs to treat it. The memoirs that flood our bookstores can become little else than exhibitionism-by-proxy. Woundedness sells. It sells therapy, medications, and an endless preoccupation with picking our scabs, just to bleed some more. There was a time when I was part of that. Then there was a long while that I railed against it.

Now that I'm older, it makes me sad. I have seen the suffering of suffering, and I wish that it were otherwise. There are few things as pathetic as an angry old man. I'm glad not to be that man anymore, and it still embarrasses me to think how long my mutineer mentality lasted. It ended, I hope, right on time.

Freed of my pathology of woundedness, but still wounded, my point of view is different. Yes, bad things have happened. Everyone is wounded now. Allen Ginsberg said, "It isn't enough for your heart to break because everybody's heart is broken now."

James Hillman—psychologist, scholar and founder of post–Jungian archetypal psychology, and creator of the acorn theory of character—said in an interview, "It's a worldwide myth [that says] each person comes into the world with something to do and to be. The myth says we enter the world *with a calling*" [emphasis added by author]. Hillman says that there is a "daimon" that chooses the egg and the sperm. Indeed?

There is something that precedes our being? Some mythical and irreducible seed that chooses to come into life, and in the form of an individual being?

Yes, if you choose to accept the myth. Remember, once again, that this is a myth, a teaching story, a latticework based in centuries of the human urge toward wholeness and awakening, upon which we can trace the internal narrative of our lives, lives that are chosen by a guardian angel. Hillman assures us that this angel inhabits us and has our best interests at heart.

I choose to believe this myth, and I have found it illuminating to consider my life in its wisdom. I believe that there is a guardian angel who has accompanied me all of my life. What I do not believe is that I necessarily was forced, through some sort of divine conscription, to follow this angel's urgings. I might have missed them entirely, and I damned sure tried to drown them for many years.

## Interlude

During basketball practice one night in Nashville, Tennessee, in the winter of 1959, I had a story moment worth retelling and remembering. Collecting these moments is how I've learned to put my life together under different lights and to pull back those parts of myself I thought were lost.

As usual, the high school varsity players all went to a local drugstore before practice and ate french fries and sweet pastries and drank cherry Cokes. The varsity practice began at 4:30. We wore Chuck Taylors, fashionable long before our time. I was a senior and not much of a basketball player. I was the sixth man on the team, at best, and was notable only for being able to take rebounds away from boys much taller than me. I always knew where the ball would be and got there and brought my elbows into play. I could jump higher than my six-foot-two would indicate, and I was mean and aggressive. The right place, the right time, the right attitude and altitude.

We were taking shots before practice formally began. I was deadly from the top of the key and was lucky to get near the hoop from anywhere else. This was a slow and lazy time, as practice approached and the french fries began their waltz with the sugar and carbonation.

A fellow walked into the gym, down at the far end, coming from the general direction of the boys' locker room. He was average height, dressed in fashionable clothes more suited for the stage of the Grand Ole Opry than a private school gymnasium. His light-colored hair was very long and was combed up and back, and it had the effect of making his head into a small thing, with a thin nose and piercing eyes, meant only to support such hair. Boys didn't wear their hair like that in 1959. That would come four or five years later. Normal high school boys just didn't do it.

But Phil Everly did.

Phil walked in and sat, watching us shoot. We shot, watching Phil sit, watching us. My friend John Booker, who had attended every one of the Everly Brothers' recording sessions, waved to Phil and then grabbed me and said, "Hey, there's somebody I want you to meet." Phil stood as we approached. His coat was shiny, with flared tails, and he was, at that moment, the coolest guy I had ever seen. He still might be the coolest guy I've ever seen. John introduced us. I will never forget what Phil said. When I said "Hi" and reached my hand out to shake his, he took my hand in his, so bony, I recall, with a tight grip, and he said, "I'm honored to meet you." In The Voice.

"I'm honored to meet you"!!

Phil Everly? Phil Everly of the Everly Brothers was honored to meet *me?* He invited John and me to join him and his brother at the studio that night, where they were going to be recording "When Will I Be Loved?" I thanked him and said I wouldn't be able to make it, that my parents wouldn't let me stay out that late. To this day I have no idea if that was true or not.

## Memory/Story

My friend Sam Keen, the mythologist, philosopher, and trapeze artist, after listening to my long tale of addiction and woe, many years ago, just sat back with a loving grin and said, "So, what's your new story, cowboy?"

What's yours?

Here's how to uncover it, from the diamond mine/mind in which it lies, in forbidding darkness. This darkness is a good place, which we must not abandon to its often sad and thankless tasks. This is where we have put the disowned parts of our selves—not the least being the guardian angel, assumed to be a self-indulgent phantom, with no reality, no use, something left over from the magical thinking of childhood. I believe that as elders, if we are fortunate and do the work, that very mind of the forgotten child, ever present, awaits just beneath consciousness.

But first, there is what might seem to be a hazardous loose end here—a loose end, which in fact is one of the great gifts of age.

How in the world am I supposed to remember stories from my past when I can't even remember where my keys are, or where I put those photographs I took over at New Smyrna Beach a few years ago? And what about my notebook I pretend always to have with me? My luncheon dates I don't write down? That book on depression—where the hell did that get to? How depressing.

True enough, those short-term memories have checked out. However, not only is my memory for distant events hugely improved, I have also found that I remember odd bits and pieces, like quotes from poems that a few years ago I wouldn't even remember having read! Recently I found myself thinking that there was some quote from John Donne that would make a good point, but I couldn't think of it, couldn't even remember which poem it was from. So I just dropped it and moved on. When I went back to re-read my words, I found the quote, almost precisely, embedded in what I had just written. I only missed one word. (I wish I had had this problem in high school—what a great excuse for plagiarism!)

There is another piece of the "poor memory" that is important and that bears repeating, in bare words.

I am losing my mind and coming to my senses.

I find that it is not the conventional occasions—birthdays, holiday celebrations, weddings, and funerals—that lodge themselves in my mind, just beneath consciousness, erupting willy-nilly. It is, rather, the little moments that take up permanent lodging there. They are invoked by the senses, not the intellect, these pointers to deeper realities. Stepping on a stone, I am taken back to the first time I ran a measured, timed mile, on a country road with rocks and horse flop, seeing my father in the distance, standing by our 1950 Plymouth and holding a stopwatch borrowed from a storekeeper in town. It's the slant light on snow, the scent of jasmine, or the rough, wet touch of a dog's nose on my sleeping face that awaken me to my corporeal biography.

My brain, putatively the home of my mind, has lost 4½ percent of its weight since I turned fifty. Neurons in the frontal cortex have been blinking out in the motor area to the tune of perhaps 40 percent since I crossed the threshold of fifty, and there are additional losses in the visual and physical sensory part as well.

However, the intellectual areas of the cerebral cortex have clearly been going to the gym and have proven quite reluctant to leave, and these guys who remain increase their firing activity, rather than joining the outward frontal cortex neurons in hitting the road and flaming out. I also have more of certain cortical neurons, and the dendrites branching from those neurons are getting stronger by the minute.

I'm fond of my liver for its remarkable comeback, but I think my brain is the organ I'm currently proudest of. Good brain! I see now that my mind is located throughout my body. It always was, of course, but I didn't know that.

So the brain is making room, it seems, for wisdom and strength, born of experience and fed by the sensuous.

Here I am with five senses I'm certain of, plus a sixth, intuition, that I have developed beyond its normal capacity. I smell, see, touch, taste, and hear, and I believe I do it in service of the increased wisdom-making neurons and dendrites. All the science up to that last sentence is solid. The assumption that my senses serve my wisdom-making mind and brain is my preferred belief. I ask you to test it and see how true it is.

How true is the following sentence, for you, today?

*Part of me never left high school.*

I thought so.

Long-term memory is engaged in remembering the past and in calling up again those fragments of happenings we thought were isolated, which have been enriched by long experience of the world.

So it is my senses that jiggle the brain now.

I was having a blackened grouper sandwich, with fries and sweet tea, at a local coffee shop with my friend Henry, and something seemingly random about eating those fries pulled the memory joggle to call up the story about my meeting with Phil Everly in high school. This simple story took me to places I couldn't have imagined and uncovered a truth I didn't even suspect was hiding. It was a startling and finally healing revelation.

That story certainly would yield easily to the structure of pathology, compensation, and Twelve Step investigation, and is made less earthy by all.

I believe that I have spent a lifetime growing down, not up. I have moved, as best I can, toward the earth. The guardian angel seeks to come to earth and does what it can to lead me there. It is deep in the soil that I am nurtured.

Now that I am old, the walls have fallen away and the masks have turned to dust. What's left, if I'm lucky, is my true character, and my true calling, revealed. Way late, for sure, but at least I didn't successfully drown it. Carl Jung said, "The most terrifying thing is to accept oneself completely."

Meeting Everly was significant not in that I had met my first superstar, not at all. It was what he said. This young man, whom I had seen on television and whose records I had listened to, said that he was honored to meet me. That is what stuck after all these years. There was humility there, earthiness.

I saw something, I was part of a small event, and the deeper part of my soul, that part linked to my destiny and nurtured by my guardian angel, looked more deeply at the event and found the truth that longed to be expressed. I needed to be grounded, to enter the earth, humus, the humble.

Many years later, I fell to my knees in a small apartment on New York's Lower East Side, blind drunk before noon on cheap vodka bought a double shot at a time on the Bowery, and begged, "Please teach me some humility!" My guardian angel knew what I needed and forced it out of my delusional drunken mind. Two months later, I stopped drinking, all at once, and the compulsion was lifted. Then began the process of growing down.

## Interlude

I missed almost all of the second grade. I attended classes for perhaps a total of a month that year, at Crow Island Elementary School in Winnetka, Illinois. (As an aside, our milkman then was a fellow named Roy Scherer. He made movies later, as Rock Hudson.) I couldn't hear that year. I now know that I didn't want to hear the noise that The Gods—my mother and father—were making in their nightly fights. My ears were in constant pain, and many were the nights I cried myself to sleep. To this day, I have tinnitus so bad that the world of truly silent meditation is denied me, even in an anechoic chamber. The ringing is always there, exacerbated by becoming a little too intimately involved with very loud weapons while I was in the Army and with live rock-and-roll for years thereafter.

I spent the greater part of my second-grade year in bed, and most days I was left alone to care for myself. There was always plenty of ginger ale, for its mythic curative values, and there was American cheese and saltines and grape jelly, and then Marshmallow Fluff and chocolate syrup, to be combined in various ways to make "sandwiches." I wasn't allowed milk.

I sat in bed, with a glass of ginger ale with a crooked, glass drinking straw, and I read. I read for hours. I got lost in Oz and I solved mysteries with the Hardy Boys. I read comic books, too, and my favorite was Red Ryder, followed closely by Hopalong Cassidy.

I read, I fantasized, I wrote myself into these stories. For Christmas that year, I got a set of Hopalong Cassidy pistols, two of them in holsters on a leather concho belt. I was alone a lot in those days, and I found the guns and belt hidden high on a shelf in my parents' bedroom closet. There were wooden bullets. The holsters smelled of distant places, and I can smell them still today.

I fantasized. I read. My guardian angel cheered.

At night my father would often come into my room. I thought he smelled of corn, and I wondered why he was so mad at me. Now, years later, I know that stench and have smelled it on myself, and I too have expressed that rage, drunk and afraid. I cannot fault my dad, who helped me save my life, beginning in 1984, and who still, years dead, does the same. But I'm also with the poet Theodore Roethke, who wrote, "The whiskey on your breath/Could make a small boy dizzy;/But I hung on like death:/Such waltzing was not easy."

At night, then, I would read under the covers with a flashlight or, failing that, I would fantasize myself as a spectral being floating near the ceiling, looking down on the small, frightened, partly deaf child on the bed. I wonder, now, was that my daimon? I rocked myself to sleep and dreamt, and many of those dreams are with me today, and some of them inspire my work.

I sat in the bed and I read. In the printed word I found, what, escape? No, that's the pathological narrative. In the aloneness and the absorption, Destiny spoke loudly to a deaf boy.

What a gift! The illness contained the medicine. I couldn't hear and needed to be left alone. And I was given the gift of words and pictures and a growing imagination that I would not otherwise have seen.

## Growing Down

Every child fantasizes, using the material close at hand. I know that. Every child creates stories and characters to people them. I know that. But I still do it, today, at sixty-five. It began, this gift, when I was alone and fearful and, I reckon, depressed. That distant portal to my childhood has never closed entirely, and I can pass through it at any time. Such a gift!

When I was five, I was alone a great deal. We lived in Battle Creek, Michigan. I would go to the living room each afternoon, and I would build a "machine" I could walk into, and I would conduct tours, modeled, of course, on the tour I took with my parents of the Kellogg plant in that town. Again, in solitude I invented. There was no sorrow at being alone, no fear. The fear came at night, when my parents came home.

As I sat with it longer, I saw that creativity was my way out of the chaos of depression. What then of the depression? I still couldn't see it.

Carl Jung said, famously, in writing to AA cofounder Bill Wilson about an early member of AA whom he, Jung, had tried to help, that, "His craving for alcohol was the equivalent, on a low level, of the spiritual thirst of our being for wholeness; expressed in medieval language: the union with God."

I confess that I used to think that was so much hokum. No more.

So, perhaps only eighteen months after my brief meeting with Phil Everly, and a series of misadventures with marriage and college, I had set out to drown my guardian angel. I mistook spirits, outside of me, with Spirit, indwelling. I drank, I used drugs, and I spent my life in an orgy of reckless abandon. My isolation deepened. I disowned the part of me that would protect me. I believe that it was always there, and that, finally, in one brilliant moment, it triumphed.

My life, without an understanding of my destiny, was one of isolation, confabulating, and, in AA parlance, "the paralysis of analysis" and "geographical cures" (running away from home it was called, but running *to* home is what it was).

With my knowledge of my destiny, my life was one of standing apart and watching, of making a story through the connections I saw, and of wandering, looking for a sense of place and raw stuff of story. Looking for home.

I'm there now. Matsuo Basho said, "Every day is a journey and the journey itself is home."

Finally, I saw that the depression was always with me, and I medicated it with booze and drugs, flight and sensation. It haunted me, this curse of Saturn, the god of depression. I drowned the illness, but in doing so, I also drowned the cure. Alcohol is an anesthetic—it kills feeling. I was a born storyteller and wanderer, and yet I merely wandered and I merely lied in order to cover my tracks. I was a tourist on the earth and in my own life.

Through retracing my life story and casting it in the light of the guardian angel narrative, I could begin to awaken to my deeper destiny.

At no point in my life was the presence of the angel more vivid, in retrospect, than on that morning in 1984 when I awoke, brutally hungover, and discovered that, in the blackout of the day and night before, I had found a story about the storyteller and poet Raymond Carver and had left the magazine open, next to my coffee pot, so I would be sure to read it on that destined morning. It was a story of a man who had quit drinking and had released the power of his imagination in ways that had always impressed me deeply. On that day, an accomplished storyteller passed the message of destiny to a nascent and still struggling one. How was it that I had found that story the night before, in a total blackout? How had I known that I needed to read it, but that I had to be somewhat clear-headed to do so? Something worked in me, with my best interests at heart. I have not had a drink since that day.

For the first time in the course of writing this book, I saw a link. I was a lifelong depressive. Or so I opined, but I knew I would need other opinions on the matter, and a year later, I finally got them.

That's pathology, the way I've written about it. But now let me add the guardian angel narrative—what happened in me to banish the shadow of these moods. I saw that throughout my life, during times of depression, I would "escape" into storytelling.

That is *not* escape. It is not moving away from depression; it is moving toward my destiny. And so I looked at the depression differently. Here was my great wound, the wound through which God could enter.

In the service of transparency, I did consult with those who know better about such depression. They offered options; I chose to go ahead as I was going. I also spoke with my friend Bruce Branin about it. Bruce is the one who told me that I wasn't wrong to grow old. This time he said, "You don't want to get too well!" Right on, Bruce.

I renamed my depression, far more accurately. It was a melancholic state of mind, a way of seeing the world in its fragile beauty, which makes it all the more beautiful still. The reality of impermanence makes it all so wondrous.

There is a lesson here, which came to me late.

It was relayed by a dear friend of many years, who told me, "There are many things in life that will catch your eye, but only a few will catch your heart. Pursue those."

I always wrote and told stories, from earliest childhood. I have wandered far in my life, never staying put for more than a few years. I enjoy being alone and I revel in making connections where others might only see isolated events. That is not sickness—not for me it's not. It's health and wholeness. I wander. I tell stories by making connections as I sit in solitude. That's what's true, freed of my ordinary pathological mind-set. Once I had seen that central truth, there was only one left to dismantle. And then I set out on this new, elder path, which I am on today.

So, what is your path? What catches your heart?

## *Interlude*

Lillis McElroy was born in Center Point, Texas, on August 18, 1886. Her mother was Kate Nowlin, born in 1864 in Kendall County, Texas, and died in Center Point in 1901. Her father was James Lafayette McElroy, born in Tennessee in 1858 and died in Center Point in 1929. He was a Texas Ranger. After Kate's death, James married Alice Powell (1868–1966) in 1904. She is also buried in the Center Point Community Cemetery.

In 1902, Jim Alexander, a practicing physician from McKenzie, Tennessee, came to Center Point to take the cure for tuberculosis. Many such folks came there for that purpose. The locals called them "lungers." Jim died there. His brother, Marvin, also a physician and also from McKenzie, went to Center Point to see to Jim's affairs and with the intention of settling down. He did not. He did, however, meet the sixteen-year-old Lillis. They fell in love. Marvin was born in 1878. According to Lillis, "I was forbidden to write (to Marvin) etc., etc., they said he was too old for me, was taking advantage of me, etc., etc."

Lillis was in college in San Antonio when she turned eighteen, on August 18, 1904. She told her parents she was "free, white, and eighteen," and on August 19, she married Marvin and dropped out of college. By August 21, they were in McKenzie, where Marvin resumed his practice and where they had four children: Lloyd, Kate, Harry Lee, and James. I have written much of this book sitting in Marvin's rocking chair. (More about that later.) He was my grandfather, and Harry Lee, my father.

Lillis was a great storyteller, and her tales of growing up in that rough section of Texas entranced me. I conflated them with the comic book stories of Red Ryder and Hopalong Cassidy. She must have known my cowboy heroes, she just must have, but I never dared ask! Lillis had the mind of a poet, and in a long letter to my aunt Lola, she told much more of the story above and concluded the part about meeting Marvin by saying, "The rest of it you know, for it has been my favorite story. I loved it all but the ending, for I'm just half whole these days." I am touched by such sentiments, deeply. Thus did people feel before we were instructed in codependency and "love myself before I love someone else."

She also made the best fried chicken I've ever eaten, with no regard whatsoever for fat and cholesterol. And creamed corn! Apple fritters! Chocolate pudding with skin on it! Black-eyed peas served with bottled chili sauce! All the vegetables were cooked with ham hocks and boiled until they had no nutritional value whatsoever, and I am convinced entirely that they were far better for this young boy than all of the engineered nutrition products in the current industrial food chain. Nowadays, I try to only eat food that Lillis would recognize as food.

When I was quite young and up to my fourteenth birthday, in 1956, I spent large parts of every summer in Tennessee. My early life was one of constant movement. From Tennessee to New Jersey to Ohio to Michigan to Illinois and finally to Florida at age eight. All those other moves preceded that one. My dad had a hard time staying employed then.

Summers, I was driven and later sent by airplane, via Memphis, to my mother's family farm in Medon, Tennessee, and would spend, as well, many weeks with Lillis in her house at 116 Magnolia Street, in McKenzie, a few hours away.

In memory, that house was a fine one. There was a deep

front porch with open railings and a classic swing (which sat three or, on a few occasions, two: me and whatever girl I wished to kiss) on one end and a glider on the other. There were a few scallop-shaped metal chairs here and there, for guests.

There were five wide concrete steps leading to the porch, and then the depth of the porch, and then the screen door, which led inside. Beyond the living room, which had also served as Marvin's office, there was a switchback staircase, with wide and well-polished banisters, which led to the second floor. I would often bolt through the screen door, swinging it as far open as I could without letting it rebound from the wall, and then run, helter-skelter, to the stairs, and up them, my hand just grazing the banister for balance. I knew, I just knew, that if I could make it all the way to the top of the stairs before the screen door slammed shut, then everything would be all right.

The right way to go to town was to turn right out of my grandmother's house, walk a block, turn left by the scandalous "modern" house, all white concrete and glass, and follow that road to the town square, where the movie theater sat at the end of the nearest side of the square.

I always went by the right way. I did that because my grandmother would be watching and would know if I went the wrong way. That was to turn left out of her house, go down a long dirt road, cross the railroad tracks (!) and then follow that dirt road all the way to the town square.

Grandmother might not be watching when I returned, so you can imagine which route I took then. I'd linger by the railroad tracks, first looking off into the distance in each direction. The rails curved out of sight going south, but going north I could see a long way. (There was a story about a boy who got caught on the rails, his shoe stuck in the switcher, and in that tale the train cut him completely in half! That was a thrilling tale. The image of the body! And where did all the blood go, so suddenly freed? The chopping sound, the gouts of blood!)

After visually scouting out the tracks, I'd crouch down, putting my ear to the rails to listen for the hum, which signaled an oncoming train. They were always humming, but I don't recall ever seeing a train close by. I'd look for the penny I'd placed on the track the week before, to see how flat the train would crush it. Never found it. The nearest house overlooked the tracks. It was decrepit, and we never saw anyone go in or out, but the grownups assured us kids that people lived there and that we shouldn't go knocking on their door. That was part of being a boy in a small town in the late forties and early fifties. There were tales in your town, too, I bet. Tales of mysterious people in an old unpainted house. Tales of children dying horribly doing things children had been told not to do.

I almost always took that wrong way home (a lifelong habit, I fear) and I believed that Grandmother never saw me.

I'm sure she saw me. She spent a lot of time in the kitchen, and the kitchen windows had a clear view to the railroad tracks and beyond. I'm certain she watched and, herself, listened for the sounds of an oncoming train.

I slept upstairs those hot and lovely Tennessee summers, in the room at the front of her house in McKenzie with dormer windows that opened onto the roof. Sometimes, very late at night, I would carefully open the window and go out and sit on that steep roof and look at the stars.

The bathroom was at the other end of the hall and was directly above the kitchen. There was a heating vent there, under the sink. Afternoons I would go into the bathroom, quietly, and squat down under the sink and watch Lillis in the kitchen as she cooked. She was a sorcerer, an alchemist, who took dead things and green things and liquid and powders and mysterious handfuls of flakes and seeds and created nourishment. Not only in the kitchen did she create nourishment, my friend. Not only in the kitchen.

Her concentration was complete. I could not have been happier if Buster Brown and Tige had been cavorting in the kitchen.

Grandmother let me help her cook. I carried things from place to place and stirred things. One mercilessly hot afternoon, when the sun was just a mile away, I was standing at the sink, washing some pots. I was ten years old and felt useful and loved.

To my right, about four feet away, was the Frigidaire. A

man came, once a week, with a big block of ice, held in tongs, resting on a horse blanket over his shoulder, to put in that white enamel box.

Between the sink and the Frigidaire there was a large rotary fan with steel blades. Stand, shaft with motor, whirling blades, rotating. True simplicity. I was washing the pots. Just outside the window was the sandbox where I played when I was much younger. I used Ajax soap and a white dishrag. I was thirsty and grandmother was on the porch off the kitchen doing something, I don't know what. I figured I could sneak a Coke. There were always squat bottles of it on the top shelf of the Frigidaire. I moved to my right a bit and, keeping my eye on Lillis, I reached for the door to the Fridge.

The noise was loud, the chunking sound of meat being chopped and bone broken, the blood was copious, and my holler insistent and long, as I stuck my finger into the rapidly whirring blades of that steel fan. My right index finger. There are three large scars on it to this day and it ain't shaped right.

I was in pain, I was very frightened as I couldn't see the finger for all the blood, and I felt faint.

But above it all, I felt my lifelong fear, one that I have to this day. I'd been found out. I'd been found out, and Grandmother would see me as a failure and a thief, and I was ashamed.

Not to be.

Lillis rushed in and held me for a moment and then looked at the bloody finger. She wiped it clean with her apron. You could see the bone. She held my arm up in the air and walked me back into her bedroom and on into the bathroom. It smelled of lilac, of Grandmother. She got out a very complete first-aid kit from Grandfather's old doctor's desk, and she fixed that finger up just fine, and all along she said, "Don't worry, Billy, you'll be OK." I felt loved and safe. Such is "grandmother mind," not blaming, but nurturing and nourishing. And just so, on that day, in the presence of Lillis and blood and pain, the daimon stirred. That part of me that has become so important in my later years awoke, and it took Lillis to awaken it. Lillis, that is, and those blades, and a reckless ten-year-old boy.

# The Mind of My Grandmother

There are three objects on my desk, other than the requisite electronic gadgets. One is a large left-handed conch shell, the size of a child's catcher's mitt, and another is a horse head about seven inches tall, with arched neck and ropey withers, exquisitely carved in blond wood. Both of those were gifts from my son. The third is a picture of Lillis McElroy, my paternal grandmother. She is wearing three strands of pearls over a collared dress, which is pale green with a paisley design. She is wearing glasses with yellow-tinted lenses. She is smiling. It's a rare smile. Most often pictures of folks carry a message of "look at me!" Mine certainly do, the gods know. The rare person, like Lillis, seems to be saying, "Well now! Look at you!" Her hair is white, as it always was in a small boy's mind, now sixty-five, and it is wispy.

I keep the picture there to remind me of three important realities in my life as I grow older. One is to remember the Tibetan idea that everyone we meet was once our grandmother in another life. Another is to try to be in touch with my own "grandmother mind." And, finally, and most important, to remind me that my past is not always what I think it is. That has been the reality that has driven the writing of this book, and no one reminds me of that better than my grandmother. As I get older, I see my past through different eyes and can see with gratitude how it was shaped and how, I now believe, I was in the care of a power greater than myself, within myself, which I think of as my guardian angel. Occasionally, that angel would take human form, and it never did so more brilliantly than with my grandmother.

My grandmother encouraged me to take risks and to play make-believe. I played by myself most of the time. I didn't know what it was to be lonely. I was content by myself, weaving dreams and telling stories. Yet another life-long habit. I had cousins in town, but we would only get together on weekends for meals and sometimes in the evening. I became creative at my make-believe. Lillis was a wonder then. She'd help me make a multipurpose cape, for Captain Marvel, Superman, and, most often, Batman. No

Robin—this was a true bachelor Batman, unencumbered. She'd caution me not to climb the railings and "fly" off the porch, and I'd do it anyway. But you knew that.

It was Lillis who showed me the joys of poetry and who taught me to respect books, the physical objects themselves. The first poet I remember reading was Ogden Nash. The first poem of his I remember was about Tibet, and a lama. It was magic to me. I have traveled in the Bhutanese Himalaya, just below Tibet and contiguous with it, and that poem, decades and decades after I read it, would surface from time to time through the porous membrane, for which I am grateful, which separates my childhood from the adult years.

Lillis's husband, Marvin, died when I was seven, and my only memories of E. Marvin Alexander, M.D., are of his bulk and of the sweet smell of the cuspidor that sat beside the very rocking chair in which I now sit, writing these words. I was given over to the tender mercies of Lillis, and she did well. She did well what I see now as the task of an elder. To become rooted and to forget the self and to see the souls of the younger ones, whether related by blood, circumstance, or mere sociability, and to quietly encourage the birth of those souls. With my son and with many other younger people in my life, I do not teach—on a good day. Neither do I argue, persuade, point out, or otherwise be didactic. What I do try to do is to invoke their own guardian angel. To see it rising and to call it forth in subtle ways so that it can do its work. That is often not the job of a parent. Parents get a bad rap in this culture of "nature or nurture." We feed, shelter, clothe, educate, and protect these children, and that alone is a lot.

We need grandmothers on every street corner, in every classroom, at the entrance to every public building.

Grandmothers aren't necessarily women, in this case, and they aren't even necessarily elders. But the latter helps!

So what is it that Lillis did, really, in the light of what I know today?

Lillis McElroy *saw* the small boy, given over to her care in the Tennessee summers of the 1940s and 1950s. Every being yearns to be seen. I was. My grandmother had no agenda for me. She was responsible; that is, she responded to what she saw in me, a vision born of her own compassion and equanimity.

When I revisit those moments, I see, from this great distance, that my childhood was not entirely what I thought it was, a time of constant travel and vast loneliness. It was a time, as your childhood was as well, when my daimon, another good word for guardian angel, was protecting me and providing me with nourishment for the man I would become.

When Lillis bandaged my finger that I'd cut on a fan blade at age ten, I saw and internalized that when a child is hurt and frightened, he must be nurtured rather than shamed. I saw a healer at work. And I wanted to be one.

That is a task that cannot be completed, and I think it is largely a task of the elders.

In 2006, the poverty rate for minors in the United States was 21.9 percent—the highest child poverty rate in the developed world. That's nearly one out of every four. Every day children are born into homes where addiction and violence poison the daily stew.

Children are sent to school to learn, in order to compete, in order to be sent to war or to contribute to the GNP. Is that OK with you? No wonder the Harry Potter books and the *His Dark Materials* trilogy were so popular. Here were children, supported by grandmothers in many guises, sorcerers, say, and great white bears, declaring, "I'm going to school to learn magic and to solve great mysteries. The world hurts, children are dying, and I want to know why!"

Lillis let me play and make mistakes and take risks and be a proper boy at a proper time. She had no plans for me beyond any one day. In the heat of Tennessee summers, amid pots and pans and the distant call of the train, going by twice a day, she lived as the great teachers would have us all live. She lived in the present moment, with love and compassion and joy. In her world, there was no one to blame, no one to "mold," no one to dominate with the "will to power." The spirit of the young girl from Texas enlivens me to this day. All these years later, I tell stories, I write poems and read the world's poetry, and I try to heal the wounds that I've caused and the ones that others have suffered at the hands of yet others.

We need grandmothers in every classroom, in every corporate boardroom, in every church, temple, and zendo.

We need, that is, selfless compassion. It can be for the one grandchild in your life or for the children in the neighborhood, the starving children worldwide, or the children of addicts. And certainly we can be grandmothers to the addicts themselves, letting go of the nastiness of "take the cotton out of your ears and put it in your mouth," by saying, "Please, tell me your story and I'll tell you mine." We can be grandmothers to the checkout clerk at the market, one of my favorite grandmothering skills, and to the anxious student butting ahead in line at the coffee shop, late for class.

The whole world is full of grandchildren. Let's us—you and me—learn to be grandmothers.

Eihei Dogen, the putative founder of the Soto Zen sect in Japan, some 800 years ago, said, "You can understand all of Buddhism, but you cannot go beyond your abilities and your intelligence unless you have *robai-shin,* grandmother mind, the mind of great compassion. This compassion must help all of humanity. You should not only think of yourself."

Indeed. I can understand all of the Twelve Steps, or the Catechism, or St. Paul, but without grandmother mind, I am, to quote Paul, "a noisy gong, a clanging cymbal."

Thanks, Lillis. Thanks for your teachings, still alive today.

## Interlude

When I was a child in rural Tennessee, I got up early and milked the cows and then saddled my horse and rode out with my uncle to check crops—cotton, corn, soy—or to move sheep or cattle from one pasture to another. Afternoons were mine, and I would ride my horse over the seemingly endless acreage of this huge farm. In the far pastures I would ride at a full gallop, standing in the stirrups. And there was a pond I would visit, where I would let the horse rest and sit with my feet in the cool water and watch the long-legged bugs skitter on the surface and run my hand across the silt below and watch the slow way that it created great amoebic forms and then settled again.

These were days of awe and wonder. Yet in the very first of those years, there was violence and fear and rootlessness. My father drank. As I explained earlier, we moved, in my first seven years, from Tennessee to New Jersey to Kentucky to Ohio to Michigan to Tennessee again and to Illinois and finally to south Florida, where I began the third grade. I was a child of the road.

In the background of the movement, as a child, was a sense of not belonging. I was very skinny as a young boy, and tall. In elementary school, I was called "Daddy Long Legs."

In my teen years, there was still awe and still some wonder at it all. My brother was born when I was twelve. There was something miraculous about that to me, and I was his constant caretaker for many years. But in the background there remained the violence, the rage, and the sense of not being quite enough.

Then, at fourteen, I drank. By fifteen, I had found safety and comfort.

The silken net of isolation began to wrap around me, and I moved apart from you, from everyone, from love.

# Rocking Chair

I have written much of this book with a fountain pen, on yellow legal pads, sitting in a rocking chair. I have three such chairs. Two of them are from L.L. Bean—one is the famed "Presidential Rocker" and the other is a porch rocker that I keep in my family room. They are both perfectly serviceable chairs; good for guests or for lazy reading when I've a mind to do so.

It's the third chair where I have done this writing. It was built in Tennessee, circa 1890, of quartersawn oak, a material that hasn't been used for decades. It is *ur*-rocker, graceful and comfortable, and its years have given it a deeper grace and provide me spiritual comfort. It belonged, at first, to Lillis's husband, my grandfather, Marvin Alexander, who died when I was seven. My only memories of him are suspenders and cigars and a spittoon that sat beside this very chair. When I was little and he was still alive, it was a great privilege to go into his home office and sit in this chair. I was too small to really rock it very well; it's a big chair, and I was a skinny little boy, engulfed in man-scented leather and wood.

Over the years, the chair gave out. The cheap leather seat and back cushions frayed, dried, and finally cracked, deep fissures that exposed rusted steel springs. My father had it, here in this very house and in every house he ever lived in. It was his chair, and no one else could sit in it.

When dad died, it became mine, and it is a repository of even more stories now. Many people have sat in it with me. Jimmy Buffet, Stephen King, Elvis, Gabriel García Márquez, Lorca, Eliot, and many more, all have sat here with me. Beethoven and Son House have entertained me, and I have sat in the chair alone, and I have cried, sitting in that chair, comforted by story. I am not the only one to have done so.

In spring of the year 2000, I had the most painful moment I had yet experienced in fifty-eight years of living. I picked up my son at school—he was ten—and I took him to a park bench beside a beautiful pond in exurban New Jersey. I had told him earlier that day that I would pick him up, in our 1989 Ford F-150, a truck we both preferred over my fancy new Dodge truck with some aggressive name, belching testosterone, slippery with power, deep blue, and menacing.

We sat for a while and we looked at the pond, and then I told him that his mother and I were not going to be living together anymore.

It is not easy to see a heart break. He said, "You're kidding, right?" I said that I wished I was, and tears came into his eyes and his face flushed, and I saw the genuine face of unguarded and astonishing grief. We sat for a while, and I told him the story that his mother had agreed to, reluctantly, that she was unhappy and felt that I was the cause of the unhappiness and wanted me to leave.

We sat some more. His mother and I had a plan. While I was telling Will this sad news, she would tell her three children, whom I had helped raise. I would show Will my new house and then take him to the home that was no longer mine.

I had already bought a house, you see, and had moved furniture into it and, on that very day that I told Will what had happened, I had moved all of my books and other paraphernalia out of what was now his mother's house.

I had put the rocking chair in the back of my F-150, wrapped it in blankets and laid it on its side, and moved it into the new house.

The house was not new. It was called the Widow Ralston House, and it had been built in 1860 by the widow of one of the original settlers of Mendham, New Jersey. It was red with yellow trim and sat on a full acre almost in the middle of town. There were old apple trees, and most of the lot was left wild. The old barn was now a garage. It was old, defiantly old, and full of stories. It was surrounded by grotesque McMansions, which that part of New Jersey is, shamefully, known for. These were 10,000-square-foot houses on mini-lots. My old house stood out like a halo in the Ninth Circle of Hell.

I drove Will over to see it, in that old truck. When we pulled into the driveway and parked by the barn and he saw the house, he said, "It's almost worth it."

"Old" does that like "new" never will. There is more comfort in worn wooden counters, rich with the patina of age, and handmade nails, crooked and rusty, than there can possibly be in the glitzy Formica and perfect tenpenny nails, hammered with machines by indifferent builders, eager to move on to the next new house.

We went into the house and I showed him the stairs from the basement, open to the parking area, up to the first floor. They were worn and curved down by 140 years of footfalls. The dining room had a fireplace, the living room a nonworking wood-burning stove. Upstairs, my bedroom had another wood-burning stove that would heat the entire house, I discovered the next winter, a particularly bitter one. Will's room was small, with oddly shaped windows, and I saw he felt comfort there. There was an old dresser, painted, poorly, bright blue, which had belonged to his maternal grandmother.

In the living room, next to the stove, sat his great-grandfather's rocking chair. After the tour was over, he went straight to it and sat and looked out the window for a while.

I knew his mind then, and I know now that that old house was a great blessing. It gave him, and me, far more ease of being in these awful circumstances than one of the McMansions ever would. I've been in those homes and you probably have, too. My experience of them is similar to the experience of snorting coke. I get high and disoriented and am thrilled with the surface of things: the polish and the vast rooms with perfect furniture, manufactured to look old. In the Widow Ralston House, that day, there were stacks of books, Will's and mine. In the McMansions? Shelves upon shelves of books, in manufactured libraries, bought by the yard, with perfect leather bindings, never read. My books were old by use, with pages turned down and underlining and torn covers. I had read them, most of them. I know, for certain, that the books bought by the yard were meant to convey a sense of "old" that screamed folly to anyone who knew how to listen.

I have a young friend who grew up in one of those houses. The perfectly manicured five acres, with transplanted old trees and gardens carefully tended by "the help," were fenced and gated. Deer were not welcome, and you had to ring a buzzer at the gate and announce yourself to get into that place.

It was beautifully decorated. Beautiful as if Ralph Lauren and Martha Stewart, those grand artificers, our cynical creators of false appearances, had dropped some particularly toxic LSD 25, broken out the cheap white wine, and had at it, naked and slack, for a debauched weekend, cackling and weeping as they ordered about a crew of carpenters, furniture designers, painters, spacklers, and paper hangers and then had slinked off, at dawn, with a box of money.

My friend said that she grew up in "a house that felt like no one lived there."

Our longing for the superficial qualities of "old" is great, but that manufactured genteel life creates suffering. Longing for the comfort of old, we build a simulacrum and move in and never touch it, and we are haunted, I believe, by the absence of ghosts. We surround ourselves with unread books and scent the air with candles meant to suggest tobacco and leather, and never smell the rich scent of the person next to us in bed, night after night, alone in a deadly carnival land.

I'll take Granddad's rocking chair and my eclectic collection of books, piled here and there, any old time.

On that sad day, Will sat and he rocked in the chair, and I sat on a sofa nearby where he could see me from the corner of his eye, but I left him alone, deep in the chair, deep in his grief.

We spent over two years in that house. We left our small acre wild, but planted flowers around the apple trees. We had a hammock. We played football and catch in the small piece of manicured lawn. During that time, Will told me that he was sick of the "F. S.," his way of describing the suburbs and of going to a school where everyone went home at night over a radius of fifty miles. He told me he wanted to move to New York City with me and go to public school and have friends to hang out with in a real neighborhood, with old coffee shops to go to after school. His mother agreed, and we spent days poring over maps and weekends walking the crooked old streets of the West Village and SoHo. We found a place in Tribeca (a beautiful and very "in" neighborhood) and I agreed to make an offer the next day.

The next day was September 11, 2001. The very new collapsed horribly into the old streets that surrounded it. One of those streets, Vesey Street, was the one our apartment-to-be was on.

Time passed in slow motion in our little commuter town.

Will ended up going to boarding school in New England, our oldest European settlement. At Milton Academy, he was in the same dorm that T. S. Eliot lived in when he was a student there. Old.

The chair and I moved to Florida. I had it rebuilt and reupholstered. The man who did it was ninety-one years old and long retired. He only worked on old things, lovable things, and this chair was one of them. I watched him work one afternoon. He was slow and loving and methodical. Once he just hunkered back on his heels and looked at the chair in deep admiration. It took him a full month to make that old chair not into something new, but into a dignified, regal, and comforting old thing, dense with story.

Another story, created from that one old chair.

But our old people? We've become burdens—in the past, to be warehoused or condescended to or occasionally propped up and talked to. Our stories are locked inside, even as we sit in that rocking chair, or rest our hands on that sideboard, or fling our hats at the hall tree our ancestors used, a century before.

The stories atrophy and are lost.

Here's what I did with my parents. I taped them telling stories about their lives. There were many memories. All I had to do was shut up, for once, and listen. I asked them about the people, places, and things they most valued. A few examples: For my mother, it was the wagon they'd hook the horses to, to go into town and then get on the train for a weekend trip to New Orleans. For Dad, it was the single-horse buggy that his father, Marvin, would get into late at night when a runner had come to tell him that someone had cut off a finger or that this other one was having a baby and it was breech; and later it was the first Model A Ford in McKenzie, his dad's. For Mom, it was the clotheslines in the backyard in Medon, Tennessee, and the rifle a distant relative, long dead, had used in the Civil War. And for Dad— for Dad it was this very rocking chair I'm sitting in now, writing to you.

What is your "Grandfather's rocking chair"? What is the one thing that, if you let it, will tell you stories? Not your iPod, I reckon.

Will you ask your children or a friend to let you talk into a video camera and tell your stories? Are those the stories you value, or would you rather they remember the stories told by our designated storytellers in Hollywood?

When my son is here this summer, we plan to film me, sitting in the rocking chair.

That's where the stories are, and I, for one, will not let them die untold.

You?

# Forgetting

*"Let us be silent, that we may hear the whispers of God."*
—Ralph Waldo Emerson

# Silence

If it is our busyness and internal noise that keeps us from seeing the face of God, and if it is only in the acknowledgment of our essentially sacred nature and the sacred nature of all things that we can be useful, then what is the antidote to the busyness and the noise?

To inhabit silence. More specifically, it is to court silence in the outer world and to move into it in the inner one, through meditation. Prayer comes into it as well, but with great restraint. Thomas Merton specifically warns about prayer in the context of the meditative life, where certain practices can actually be counterproductive and lead inexorably to the "dark night."

It is in silence, rightly cultivated, that our memories gestate and become the stories that rise to our consciousness as the beacons of truth held up by our guardian angels. It was in that silence that I learned my destiny as storyteller.

Throughout the centuries, from beginningless time, people have sought the solitude and silence of remote places. The Christian Mount Athos, in the Aegean, is the centuries-old center of Orthodox Christianity. The monastic community there lives in silence, as does the community at Father Thomas Merton's home monastery, the Abbey of Gethsemani in Kentucky. The early Christian Desert Fathers knew that only in such an imposing and difficult place could they pray the Gospel. In a brilliant movie called *Amongst White Clouds,* we are given at least superficial access to the lives of hermit monks in China's Zhongnan Mountain range, who work and study and sit for hours in the solitude of these mountains. The legendary Taoist sage Wang Ch'ung-yang, when called to become a teacher, feigned illness and locked himself in his study for twelve years to sit in the silence of the Tao.

According to Father Thomas Keating, the migration of thousands of young people to India in the sixties and seventies, which he speculates was encouraged by the Second Vatican Council, was a turning point in our culture, with prayer and meditation in the ascendant. In his teaching on contemplative prayer, we are given the opportunity to remember our original nature, that of union with God, through prayer first, then reflection, and, finally, with an opened heart.

For the past few years, I considered myself to be a recovering Buddhist. For many years, I practiced only the form of Buddhism and missed the point. I have continued to meditate and to study Eastern ways of thinking, and I have a teacher, but I don't have a name for what I do. I suspect that as time passes, I will give up that conceit as well.

I tell you that by way of saying that, in what follows, I will speak of God, of the Buddha (who was, after all, only a man), and of various other manifestations of the divine. I am comfortable in doing that, although if I had to declare my position I would say, today, that I am by a narrow definition an atheist. As my friend Chris Coates puts it, "You're an atheist who goes to church and prays. I don't get it." Here it is: I do not see God, the divine, as an external and transcendent being. The divine is within, just as suggested in the book *Alcoholics Anonymous,* where we are told: "We found the Great Reality deep down within us. In the last analysis it is only there that He [sic] may be found." I believe that Jesus was a great Yogi, as was the historical Buddha, who was, in fact, one of millions of Buddhas. Buddha is reading these words, right now. The names we give to the divine are convenient, but they are limiting. The point is that it is our nature to seek this divinity and that, finally, it can only be found within. I do not believe in external, separate, creator God, but I do have confidence, based on the experience of the centuries, that I contain the seed of the divine, and that if I only can turn off the eternally "selfing" small mind, I can experience it directly.

As I have aged, I have had the gift of an ongoing sundering of the social chains that bind me. I have lost much of the vanity of the perpetual adolescent, although I still check myself out in every mirror I pass. I am less likely to be disturbed by negative things said to me about me, and I am generally unshaken by behavior of others that I may consider less than beneficial. Sometimes. Living meditatively is easier now than it has ever been. I'm not proud that I had to wait until all the processes slowed down before I embraced it entirely, but that is what is.

The opportunity to live the contemplative life is always there. One needn't be aging to wish to approach and embrace it.

But it's easier now, isn't it?

And it's *essential* if we are to be of maximum service and if, in that practice, we are to raze the false assumptions about aging and death.

To continue the addict's life of "Bisy Backson" is deadlier now than ever.

And the lives of the Taoist "immortals" or the Desert Fathers or the monks on distant mountains are not for us.

(It was my fantasy for years that such would be my destiny, but no thanks.)

We inhabit a soundscape, longing for silence. The soundscape is vast and textured, noisy and soothing. A lover's murmur is sound. So is the music on the stereo in the car next to you at the stoplight, shaking that car and your own. When my son, Will, says, "Good night, Dad, I love you," sound is holy and laced with hope. When the talking head on the news talks of the latest bloody happening in this blood-soaked world, the sound is exploitive and shrill—a gift to the masters of the corporate technological world. Will's "I love you" opens a mojo of care and connection; the TV news noise awakens my sixties Marcuse-quoting twin, who is only just resting before the revolution comes around again.

But, in reality, sound does not have meaning; we give meaning to it. Sound can arise as speech, as music, as environmental noise, in any one of myriad vessels. But it has no intrinsic meaning.

I was once backpacking with my stepson, deep in the Big Sur wilderness. We were miles from the persistent hum of civilization, sleeping in our tent on a spring night, with the Little Sur River just a few feet away, beyond the circle of our sputtering fire. David was eight. All night long, when I would come out of my sleep, I was aware of the uneven guttural sound of the rushing river water as it pounded in the hollows of rocks on the other shore. It was an uncanny sound, deep and resonant beneath the playful sibilant splashes of water in the deeper courses in the middle of the river, slipping over waterfalls just upriver.

At dawn, in the cold, I got up and started the little Svea stove to make hot tea and then oatmeal, with raisins and honey. I squatted in my shorts and sweatshirt and heavy boots by the remains of the fire, the stove on a rock. I heard David come out of the tent, head back into the woods for a moment and then rustle out to the fire pit. He squatted beside me, tousled.

"I'm glad the bears stayed on the other side of the river," he said.

There are no bears in that part of Big Sur that I am aware of, so I was really puzzled. When I asked what he meant, he said that he heard them during the night, grumbling, just on the other side of the river. I said I hadn't heard them, that the bears were much farther north and at higher altitudes. He insisted. So did I.

Then I understood and I asked him if he still heard them. He listened for a moment and said, with a puzzled smile, that yes, he did.

I led him across the river on a massive pine bridge, the remains of a tree felled in a storm I'm glad I missed. We looked at the water as it pounded against the hollows and listened to the "bear" sounds. He reckoned that that was it, and we scampered back across the log and cooked some oatmeal and had sugar cookies and tea.

We both needed to give meaning to an unknown sound. Even if that sound was frightening. I wonder what "bear" was to David at eight? A grizzly, like one he might have seen, dead and mock ferocious, in some Western town? Or one that, on better days, sounded like Phil Harris, the voice of Baloo the bear in Disney's *The Jungle Book*?

Here's what else I like to wonder or, better, imagine.

Were there some bears there during the night, their sounds blending with the musical rocks?

Unknown things lurk just outside the campfire's light, seen only as darker places in the already dark canvas of nighttime canyons or desert vastness. Something rustles and moves, and there is a darker, moving place, in the dark.

We are meaning makers, and sometimes we make meaning at the cost of awe and mystery. David needed to understand that noise, and I was pretty sure that I did, after some thought.

In all the silence of that night in the canyon by the river, we listened for the familiar in the unknown. And the silence enveloped us finally.

We live in a soundscape—a soundscape that includes our stories.

Its background is silence. Silence gives birth to the soundscape and the soundscape returns to silence. Silence is a basic phenomenon. Unlike other phenomena, it is causeless and, furthermore, contains the others. In Buddhism, we might say that silence is emptiness; in Christianity or Judaism, that silence is God. Silence is that from which everything is born and to which everything returns. Edgar Allan Poe says, "Silence, which we call quiet, is the merest word of all." The word indicates something we cannot directly experience; our experience of silence is entirely in the relative, not the absolute, realm.

In a hidden monastery in the mountains near Paro, Bhutan, in March 1999, I spent a day in seated and walking silent meditation. I sat and walked, slowly, in the altar room, in the company of an enormous and ancient statue of Padmasambhava, the Indian saint who brought the teachings of the Buddha to Tibet and Bhutan in the eighth century. He is still revered throughout the Himalayas as Guru Rinpoche. The statue was well over ten feet tall. Padmasambhava is usually depicted, as in this case, with upturned mustaches, a patch of chin beard, and quizzical upturned eyebrows, meeting at the bridge of his flat nose, over piercing dark eyes. His robes are silk with gold and red and orange brocade. He wears an ornate hat with upturned brims and carries implements of ritual tantric practices in his gold-painted wood and plaster hands. This particular monastery had been in continuous service for over one thousand years. The shrine room was laced with the heavy woodsy scent of Tibetan incense and lit with the guttering light of butter lamps and candles. It was musky and close. There were enormous wall hangings on every surface, depicting the Buddhist saints and their retinues in heavenly glory, and there were the wrathful deities, on red backgrounds, against brilliant blue and gold brocades, with their necklaces and headpieces of human skulls, their eyes bulging in rage, teeth bared. The stone floor, polished and worn from the footsteps and the humble bows of centuries of the devout, was cold. The presence of the divine and the sense of mystery and endless compassion were palpable.

I was alone, but for the lama, asleep in the courtyard sun, intense above ten thousand feet. My friends Brent and Sam had scrambled on up the mountain for a view of the holy mountain, Chomolhari, in the distance.

What, for heaven's sake, was an aging, rickety, confirmed Episcopalian, who had studied for three years to become a practitioner of pastoral care in that very church, doing in a place like this?

The answer is in the question. "For heaven's sake."

In some mythologies, "heaven" refers to natural process; the constant unfolding of things in the cosmological process. This is not your Father's heaven.

For a while, I had a largely uncomfortable feeling of disappearing into that place. This was not some metaphysical idea. I felt overwhelmed and lost, a stronger sensation than on hundreds of psychedelic trips. It didn't last long, but I'll never forget it. Principally, I had a sense of peace and well-being, of being cared for and of caring. I made a donation to the lama and lit the appropriate number of lamps to keep that endless flame burning.

It was not silent, of course. I heard every little sound. The mouse that was scrambling behind the altar, bird cries, and distant barks of feral dogs. I was aware of how little sound there was. The silence was filled with the present and with the ancient past. A better ear or a more creative imagination might hear the voices of the saints, static in this room, but alive somewhere. I did not. But the presence of the Buddha, of God, of the Mystery, was never more real to me, in some material place, before or since.

As my friends Brent and Sam and I walked back down out of the pass to catch our bus, eating hard, sour apples, Brent casually remarked that upon occasion, that statue had been known to speak.

It did not occur to me then and has not occurred to me since that his statement is anything other than true. There are two reasons that I believe this is entirely so. One is that there is agreement in this high Himalayan community that the statue speaks when it is necessary. Two, the statue was built with sacred intention by artisans who fully understood the power of their charge. It was built with belief in its holiness, and it is sustained, over the generations, by that same belief. It speaks. It is the reality of community and the intention of the artisans who give Padmasambhava his voice.

That voice, once agreed upon, was real, and its sound rings through the Himalayan foothills above Paro.

And yet!

This ongoing inquiry into the nature of silence and sound, and all my travels and all my reading about silence, my endless conversations with scholars and philosophers and rock musicians, and my days of quiet walking in remote places, all led to this simple understanding: You don't need to go anywhere or read anything or have great loopy wonderful conversations. All you have to do is listen.

There is a wonderful teaching story about the itinerant student who showed up at yet another monastery, carrying a bulging wool sack all full of books and notes and writing implements. He went to an interview with the master, seeking a teacher and student relationship. He went into the interview room. He bowed. He sat on the guest's cushion in front of the master. As he sat, he kept the wool sack, shifting and rustling, firmly over his right shoulder.

After he had bowed and made all the comments about his comings and goings, he asked the master to take him on as a student.

The master struck him on the hands that held the bag, and the bag fell away to the floor with a great thump and clatter.

The student was enlightened at once!

It's a good story. But I don't think that the point is that the books and papers and writings and all the utensils were of no use.

After all, that's what it took for him to be fully seen by the master. Without all the studies, this particular itinerant monk could never have become enlightened. It was his way. What was crucial was continuing the inquiry, while remaining open to whatever teachings appeared.

In the late spring of 2002, I went on retreat in Oregon. It was amazing to see how serene the retreatants were, for the most part. Not me! I was bothered. My divorce had been finalized only a few months before, my mother had died during that same month, June, and, still in June, I had turned sixty. Sixty! And I had moved from the outskirts of New York City, where I had lived for over twenty years, to a small town in Florida. I needed that internal silence more than ever. What was going on? I was getting older and nowhere at the same time! In an interview with a teacher, I told him that. I told him I'd done everything I knew to do in order to practice silence and nothing had worked. I had read about it, gone to retreats devoted to it, tried many different types of meditation, even swam daily, thinking that under water, I could . . .

He interrupted me, asking, "Do you know how to be silent?"

"No, I don't," I grumbled.

"Good. Not knowing is a profound path. Just be silent. Stop trying!"

Dammit!

I dropped the bag.

All the way home, I was haunted. Everything from "Maybe I'll become an Episcopalian again" to "My friend Elaine wants me to go to seminary; that's what I'll do" to "I have no idea what he's talking about" to "This is easy; I'll see it in no time." It was the "no idea" digression that was the important one. Entering silence isn't done by having ideas about it.

Back home, my life was in an interesting heap about my feet. It was a tidy heap, and there were very few loose ends or unresolved conflicts or even much uncertainty, beyond the usual. The country was clearly moving toward war, and the economy was a mess. I had remarked to my friend Masha in Los Angeles, "Things are awful." She said, "Yes, they always are."

My son, Will, was about to finish school and had just been accepted to Milton Academy, in Massachusetts, where he would begin studying in the fall, after a summer with his mom and then with me, picking blues on his new Epiphone Lucille model and studying kung fu and eating Krispy Kremes and sleeping late. I wasn't dating and didn't want to. I had been reading the ancient Chinese poets and found comfort in their tales of reclusive later years. Sound? Silence? Solitude? How was it for T'ao Ch'ien and Han Shan? What contaminated my life? What sounds were erupting from the silence all around me?

In one instant, in that little room in Oregon, it all changed. On that day, my teacher slapped me, hard, with his one gratefully metaphorical hand, and I was stuck. I was stuck in reconstructing my past experiences, as this largely unconscious quest had unfolded, and in looking more deeply into the nature of silence.

I hope you will be able to discard these words about silence when you enter the silence itself as, gratefully, I have.

> *"There is no need to go to India or anywhere else to find peace. You will find that deep place of silence right in your room, your garden, or even in your bathtub."*
> —Elisabeth Kübler-Ross

# Big Mind

I went to Bhutan for silence; India, too, as it happens, as well as distant and exotic Oregon! And according to Elisabeth Kübler-Ross, all I needed was a bathtub. I have one of those right in my house!

Again: This soundscape we inhabit arises from silence and returns to it. Dave Brubeck is credited with saying that the real music is the silence between the notes. How did I find it, the interior silence, also arising and falling away; how did I manage to get between the notes of the ongoing melody of my life, however fitfully?

I didn't do anything; I just sat there. Finally. But in the beginning, even encouraged by the teacher's words *don't try,* I was perplexed by the "meaning" of silence.

So I finally gave up on meaning. As it turns out, that is a very good start, indeed. I began to practice creating as much external silence as I could. The television was unplugged and a large Japanese screen placed in front of it, with a life-size statue of Yoda in front of that. Television is not an enemy, at least not to me. I don't have a desire to "kill" mine, as some bumper stickers insist. I just need to let go of that part of me that's addicted to noise and movement of any kind. Bill and television together create a frightful synergy of torpor and listlessness. I stopped listening to the radio in my car, and I only play music in my home when I'm actually listening to it, doing nothing else. I was amazed to find that I, great fan of the blues, didn't know the lyrics to half the songs I had in my library. The music had been, well, background noise.

As the days turned to weeks and months, and then a year or two had gone by, something happened. I began to seek silence, more and more. Noise hurt.

Then I spent nearly a year in the jungle in Costa Rica and was without much of the noise of civilization much of the time. Night came early there, and then the critters of the jungle, from frogs to sizable cats, began their harmonizing. As the night deepened, the sounds lessened until, it seemed, the world slept.

In the morning, the howler monkeys began their very territorial New Day Symphony, composed anew every day, followed soon enough by a flight of green parrots that passed by my house each morning, at dawn, on their way from the seaside jungles to the deeper interior, to feed.

I had been a meditator for some time, but in this Costa Rican paradise, where the world arose and fell away every day, my meditation changed. I still took up my standard posture every morning, but I was casual about it. I was still but not rigid. Sitting in meditation was no longer a contest, a samurai exercise in manly serenity. I became softer and gentler and, occasionally, as I sat, there was only the jungle and its sounds and movements, the winds pushing the flowers around, rustling, the light growing and flowers opening. I remember now reading the Tarzan stories when I was a boy, and the descriptions of this man of the jungle, coming awake on the broad branch of a high tree and, not moving, watching a single flower open, over a long period of time. Like that.

It didn't happen often, this disappearing into the rising and falling away of the day, but it happened.

I've read that the Osa Peninsula of Costa Rica, where I lived, has the most diverse population of insects of any place on this great earth. I'm not sure if that's true, but I am certain that the majority of them came to visit me, each evening, starting at dusk, around 5:30 or so. Some nights I would bicycle into town, being careful to keep my mouth closed as I tore along the dirt road, so as not to inhale a significant portion of that diverse population. I would have some seviche at Carolina's café, hang out with my friend Hector, who was teaching me Spanish by refusing to speak English, and then I'd bike back. On the way in and the way back, I would again disappear into the phases of the meta-circadian rhythm.

Most nights, though, I would sit outside for as long as the insects would let me, usually surrounded by large frogs whom I fancied were there to provide some kind of protection, an amphibian witches' circle. Then, one would hop on my bare foot, exploding my reverie, and back inside I would scurry.

I'd sit in meditation, again. Even more comfortably than in the morning. The nighttime meditation was too edgy most of the time, as I could not accustom myself to the occasional explosions of the large owl who sat on my clothesline, hitting my screens after some moth sushi.

And so to bed, where I would drift in the diminishing breath of the world until all was silent and still.

I think of this now as dragon meditation. That is entirely my own creation and would not, I'm sure, meet with the approval of many meditation masters. It works for me nonetheless. You see, I have a tattoo of a dragon, a very large and colorful dragon, on my left forearm. Only after I got the tattoo did I set out to learn whatever there was to learn about these mythical critters. Mine is an Asian dragon, the flightless type. In ancient Chinese myth, it turns out, the dragon is the primal cause of the earth's unending cycles of arising and falling away: the cycle of birth, death, and rebirth. The dragon is not beyond this process but is, in fact, part of it, and so the dragon also is born, dies, and is reborn, endlessly. The dragon appears in the form of the blooming flower at dawn and in the death of the bloom, its transformation to earth and seed and the blooming anew. I watch the live oak trees by the creek here, from my back porch, and see the breath of the dragon moving the Spanish moss. When winter falls in my old home in the Adirondacks, the dragon descends deep beneath Lake Champlain and the ice groans with his voice as the lake goes still, and then, in spring, the dragon erupts from the surface and the winds howl again, blowing life into the trees and moving, again, the moss on the trees here and in Mallorca and beyond. The dragon's scales are the shifting tectonic plates, and his claws are lightning storms across the planet.

Fanciful? Of course. But if you can allow yourself to descend into that metaphor, you might find an interesting corollary, as I did.

Take a moment and give it a try. Now, in most books on meditation, this is the point at which the author says something like, "Just close your eyes and relax. Then imagine yourself . . ." and there follows a page or two of instructions that we are apparently expected to read, eyes closed, and practice. I won't do that. So reread the life of my mythical dragon above, and then take a seat, comfortably, perhaps on a cushion on the floor, and then and only then, allow yourself to experience, internally, the life of that dragon, however it comes up for you. Become the dragon. You will, inevitably, notice your breath.

So did you do it?

I wouldn't have either, but I'm sure you get the point.

The breath arises, the breath falls away, just like this great earth, just like your own private dragon. If not a dragon, then find your own metaphor. Once you find something that feels right, continue your practice a day at a time for ninety days. You will do it for the rest of your life!

What's the point?

As without, so within.

In this depth of concentration, the reality of the world can be experienced directly, beneath consciousness. Watching the breath, you participate in the arising, the falling away, and the arising again, of all that is. David Hinton, the brilliant translator whose words inspired this meditation, calls this "meditative dwelling in the emptiness of non-being."

Its effects for me have been to lead me to an understanding of connection and the rhythm of life that I could not have expected. And there are days when I do not have this understanding at all.

I can't summon the days when I do, but when they come, I am enriched by them.

I've left an open end here. When I first began this dragon meditation, that is not what I called it. It was Big Mind, as taught by the Zen Master Dennis Genpo Merzel Roshi, in Salt Lake City. What he has done is taken centuries of Buddhist teachings on meditation and enlightenment and created an entirely Western technology of mind to make a brilliant shortcut to the seeing through to the true self. When I think of that self, I think of it as me in the world I'm in. So, initially, when I would sit in meditation in the morning, I would make a physical shift into this Big Mind. How? Simple. I'd twist myself into the seated posture, and when I was comfortable, I would say, "I am sitting as Big Mind." Then, I would make a small shift in the posture, as minor as straightening my back, which I always need to do anyway. I'm old, I slouch! At that moment—when it works—comes the sense of vastness and connection to all that is. Without becomes within, within becomes without. No borders, no edges.

Once I understood the significance of my dragon tattoo, which was an accident, of course, I renamed "Big Mind" as "Dragon Mind." It's the same thing, the all-inclusive undifferentiated consciousness of, and in, reality—of "things as it is." (That is not a typo.)

What's important is that I can now quiet my monkey mind by simply moving out of it! With that one simple statement and that one simple actual movement. I can't think myself into Dragon Mind, but I can move there, much as I can't think myself from behind this desk to my creek-side Adirondack chair, but I can get up and walk to it.

So call this mind what you will. It's also true that I have provided myself, and you if you want to use it, with a very visual metaphor of this mind. It's important to let that go! That's the initial visualization that moves us into the mind. The mind itself has no form at all. It's not Dragon Mind and, as Dennis Merzel has said, it also isn't *Big* Mind. *Big* doesn't describe it any more than *dragon* does. It's only a metaphor and a prod to enter into the movement of what is, that movement which is, simply, the arising and falling away of the breath.

So, if you choose to try Dragon Mind, let go of the dragon and sit with the breath. There isn't anything else, and there is no goal to achieve. Just sit there!

Speaking of goals, there is no magical, one right way to enter the silence. But, in my experience and in the experience of those far, far more learned than myself, there is one way that is a setup for discomfort and, as often happens, a movement away from meditation at all. Let me be candid: There are two examples in this very book of what, in its strictest sense, is the wrong view of meditation. Twice I mention that while in deep meditation I had visions: once of a bumper sticker (how very American of me) and once of a sign. Those are projections of ego, pure and simple. They were useful, and I don't disown them. But they contaminated the meditation itself, that entering into the rhythm of "what is."

Years ago I sat with a group, once a week, in which there was much talk of enclosing oneself in a bubble of pure light or of out-of-body experiences of a profound nature. It's clear to me that most people, particularly those who are new to the freedom from addiction, would rather have an out-of-body experience than an in-body one.

I am sure that is useful, although it's not my experience. But there remains an important cautionary note. In Twelve Step programs and, more generally, in the entire culture, meditation is linked with prayer. This type of bare meditation I've outlined above is without goals, without purpose. As a brilliant meditation master I once sat with said, "It's good for nothing." So, in this one case, it is not useful to combine the meditation with prayer, especially prayer that insists on an outcome. It is also my long experience that meditating will bring wondrous results—increased focus, deeper mental concentration, and, at its most common level, a sense of well-being and connection. This type of meditation, however, is meant to illuminate the great reality of the way things are, and so to meditate with a purpose or to combine prayer with this type of meditation is self-defeating. All that is called for here is what Thomas Merton calls "simpler, more primitive." For example, "I sit as Dragon Mind." If that type of prayer is too primitive or simple, then, by all means, seek your understanding in prayer or psalms or chants.

But if you can:

Just sit!

*"The only wisdom is humility."*
—T. S. Eliot

# Resurrection

Earlier in this book, I stated that I have lived two truths. There is the truth of consensual reality, governed by desire, aversion, and folly. And there is the felt truth of my life, sensed and intuited, based in my experience. The first truth is mechanistic and stubbornly dedicated to movement and growth, like a mole, burrowing along, mindless and blind, desiring The Next, and to abundance measured in people, places, and things. It is the truth of power.

That's not "wrong" somehow, but it has outlived its usefulness, and has left us—me anyway—in a state of dissatisfaction and longing.

Longing for what?

Hold on.

The second truth is sensed and heartfelt, noticed in silence, always relative, or in the embrace of the world of the senses, all six of them. They are easily conflated. Many years ago, a lover said, "You never look at me when we're making love." True. My body was adrift in the senses, timeless, but my mind was elsewhere. I believe today that I was afraid to look at her, afraid that I would get lost and disappear into the abyss of no-self. I was judging, calculating, "working" at love and thus maintaining the myth of power, which exploits, rather than love, which nurtures. The first truth is the world of power, the second is the world of love. As you have read, it was a long time before I moved off that square on the board.

Many years ago, a monk of the Order of St. Benedict was giving me a tour, so slow, of a beautiful hermitage in the wilderness of Big Sur, California, some 1,300 feet above sea level, with the vastness of the Pacific Ocean in one direction and forests of oak and California chaparral, redwood, madrone, and bay laurel on all sides. He showed me the chapel, with its dramatic suspended cross, and walked me through the bookstore and then down to the private hermitages, for rent by week or month. He said that the endlessly gifted writer Pico Iyer came there on retreat several times a year. That impressed me! "I should come here," I thought, "and stay in one of the mobile homes and . . ." I began planning my unwritten book on silence, and except for what I've written here, it's unwritten to this day.

We finished the tour where we had started, in the parking lot outside of the main building. He thanked me for coming. I told him what my impressions of the place were, how impressed I had been by the silence, and how rare that quality is in our lives today. I mentioned the magnificent cross and opined that the monks, sitting on the small black cushions, must have felt particularly humbled by the size of it, looming there. I commented on the bookstore and showed him the books I had bought before we linked up for the tour. I had a stack of books by the likes of Brother David Steindl-Rast, who had lived there, and the great British mystic Bede Griffiths, of whom it has been said, "Bede Griffiths was a monk, a man in whom there was no guile, and was last to see the guile that may have been in any other." (His book, *Return to the Center,* still sits in my bookcase, and I might well read it some day.)

I finished sharing my thoughts with the monk and thanked him again for showing me around. He smiled. I do not recall his precise words, but I am certain they were not as caustic as my rewrite of what I heard. I heard, in undertone, and lovingly, that he hoped that I could come back some day "when you can see it."

I was a visitor from the world of power in this place of love.

So I'm stuck in this schizophrenic, your-fault, my-fault, stop-everything, Bill-needs-something-and-he-needs-it-now-and-he-is-dependent-on-you-to-get-it-and-if-he-doesn't-he-will-suffer-and-if-he-suffers-it's-your-fault-so-he-will-make-you-suffer-and-he's-right-and-you're-wrong world.

I cannot live with any comfort in the world of exploitation when I have had glimpses of the world of nurturance. As I water the seeds of nurturance, the weeds of exploitation wither. But they are always there, always prepared to bloom once more, with their dark flowers.

Awakening unfolds. In my life I have begun to move from egocentric to other-centric and, I sense, there is more to come. There is more to come when I am willing to soften and abandon my need to assign meaning or to tell myself stories, always lies, about what I now choose to see as openings to the world of spirit. I can analyze and concretize and be certain, in my endless arrogance, or I can trust my gut. It is difficult, and I become fearful of the loss of my illusory self. When fear strikes, I am diminished. When I am immersed in my senses, I catch glimpses of a larger self, encompassing all that is.

I am stubborn and delusional. Eliot says that we don't need to hear of the wisdom of old men, but of their folly, their fear. I still have that in abundance, but there is the hope, in stillness, of fearlessness.

Any spiritual experience is both the end and, often ignored, the beginning of a process. When I'm awake, I see both ending and beginning. I wonder how many I have missed.

God has some abrupt ways of getting my attention, it seems. There was a further mending of my broken-open heart on Easter Sunday in 2008.

I went to the early service at my church. I hadn't planned on going at all, but I woke early and felt that I must go. It was a cold morning, and I didn't have the top up on my jeep. The sun was just coming up, and this small town was silent as I drove the back streets, shivering in the cold of dawn.

The service was a simple one. The focus was on preparing the chapel for those yet to come on this day of resurrection and hope. My senses were alive.

The minister read from Isaiah. "Cease to do evil. Learn to do good, seek justice, correct oppression."

I remembered the Three Pure Precepts of the way of the one who is awake. "Cease doing evil; practice good; practice good for all beings."

Then came the hymn, with this verse:

"O, Jesus, you have looked into my eyes / Kindly smiling you have called out my name / On the sand I have abandoned my small boat / Now with you I will seek out other shores."

I remembered the familiar chant from the Heart Sutra: "gate gate paragate parasamgate, Bodhi Svaha." In a book that I have worked on with a calligrapher named Nadja Van Ghelue, we translated that verse as:

"Gone, gone, gone beyond, completely gone beyond, enlightenment, hail."

The original translation says, "gone, gone, gone completely beyond *the other shore*."

And it was then that I awoke to a deeper knowledge of my path as an elder.

Sitting in that pew, in that beautiful church, I put aside all that I have learned about the form of the path and began to see more clearly, in its wholeness, my true path.

The time had come (all at once, aha!) to give up all learning and to embrace the path I knew as a child, on my horse in deep woods, the path of awe and wonder and nondiscrimination, and then to embody that path for all beings. As Eliot taught, it is the path of true simplicity, costing not less than everything.

As I left the chapel, I told the minister that I had come to church expecting to take communion and, instead, had heard a call for my ministry. She bowed to me, palms together, and we held each other.

I was sixty-five years old, and I had awakened to the dreams of the Child.

Then, as fate would have it, I spoke with my friend

Gretchen. We talked of riding horses, bareback, and being one with the sound of the horse's hooves on forest paths. We spoke mere words about being completely and absolutely free, beyond words, beyond thought, absorbed in Spirit.

In Tibetan Buddhism, there is the practice of "sealing" an experience, leaving no loose ends to practices of confession or certain visualizations. It seems that I needed to seal my Easter experience.

Dreams. When I have a powerful one, scary or joyous, it's useful to write it down, if only in a sketchy form. Then I flesh it out, in the light of day, and sit with it, listen to its teachings. Here are the notes I made about a dream I had recently: "Castle. Snow. Cold. Pickup. Denny. Generous. Myshkin." I went back to sleep after making my notes, but I kept going back to one particular scene, a freeze-frame of a man I know, named Denny (not his real name), standing on a dark and forbidding curving stone staircase inside a cold and unwelcoming house and welcoming me in, with a guileless and welcoming smile.

I finally got up, let out my cat, Fred, made coffee, and fired up a Quorum Churchill (a cigar the size of a baseball bat). I sat with the dream and let my mind wander. It was four a.m. The castle in the dream was the home of people I knew only in dream time, but I wasn't welcome there, except as a supplicant. When the pickup, a beat-up old Chevy, had come up the long, steep, and winding driveway, I had hidden in some snow-covered pines, perfectly manicured. Then, as one does only in dreams, I was inside and sneaking up a cold and forbidding stone staircase from the entry hall to the upper floors. It was lit by guttering candles. Denny was just ahead of me, in khakis and a white T-shirt. I knew he knew I was there but that he was letting me get further into this unwelcoming house. After another turn in the staircase, he turned and smiled at me and said, "You don't have to hide from me." And that smile! I thought of Prince Myshkin, the hero of Dostoevsky's *The Idiot*.

Myshkin is one of the most remarkable creations in all of Russian literature, a literature that is so rich with insight and color. Myshkin is the "idiot" of the title. He lived in an asylum, considered incompetent because of his epilepsy. He is unlearned and is a truly innocent man. Leaving the asylum at twenty-six years old, he returns to Moscow. He inherits a fortune after living a life of poverty, with only one coat for the Moscow winter. But the money is unimportant to him. His suffering is great, and he is hated and feared and, in his innocence, as so often happens, he is taken advantage of. The powerful fear the innocent, and the fear turns to hate. But his innocence is more powerful than all the "passion" of those who surround him.

A spiritual mentor, Jim Morton, Dean Emeritus of the Cathedral of St. John the Divine, told me many years ago, when I talked to him about the frustrations I felt with Denny, only a boy then and precisely that innocent and misunderstood person, that the day would come when Denny would be my "greatest teacher."

Like Myshkin, who is loving and gentle, Denny has great spiritual intelligence, I now see, and does not live easily in the world of so-called passion. The villain of *The Idiot*, Rogozhin, can never forgive Myshkin for his innocence and for his refusal to live in his—Rogozhin's—world of power.

Thoreau says that love is the attempt to turn a piece of a dream into reality. Who is there, then, for me to learn to love? The sad inhabitants of that cold castle, of course. And those who exploit the guileless, as I have done so often. I must love them to love myself. They are suffering as I have. And I must learn to love the innocent, the guileless.

I have learned to pay attention to the dreams that trouble me, without interpretation. I soften, I relax, I let go, and I feel the feelings they bring up. In this case, at least, the dream proved to be a doorway into a deeper level of my subconscious, a place ever closer to my heart. And when I meet the guileless ones? I must try to see their deep spiritual intelligence and try not to be one of those who would "cure" them or shun them or exploit them. Like Denny, they can be my greatest teachers.

I believe it is a gift of age that I can begin to see that these disenfranchised ones are the avatars, the world teachers, who point to the only hope we have in these very dark ages. Listen to the poor, the guileless, the hated, and the victimized. Hear the voices of the one billion people on this planet who live on less than one dollar a day. Become them. They are you. And love those others, as well, the ones who are blinded by mere passion and a desire to dominate. Everyone's heart is broken now. Learn, above all, that within even the cruelest of us, my peers for many years, there is the heart of a child. I first heard that lesson on Madison Avenue, two decades ago with the homeless person, when Lou said, "It is always 'There go I.'"

From the moment I began this book, I have been trying to live as if my elder years were a beginning, not an ending. I have seen this as a separate life, a second and final chance to encounter the mistakes I have made thus far and to move away from making the mistakes again, but to go contrary to that useless path and see what the new path brings.

There remains the risk of analysis at any moment. I still want to ascribe slender meanings to my experiences. Even worse, I want to use the experiences as proof, somehow, of "what a good boy am I." That's the kind of behavior that would make Jesus roll his eyes in dismay or the Buddha shake his head.

"Will he ever learn? Will he ever learn to just walk the path, without analysis?"

Here's a familiar child's poem that, by my reading, points at the folly of mere understanding, based in ego:

> Little Jack Horner sat in the corner
> Eating his Christmas pie,
> He put in his thumb and pulled out a plum
> And said "What a good boy am I!"

Nope, Jack. All you did was disfigure a pie. Leave good and bad out of it.

So don't *tell* me, *show* me:

How's that pie?

# Transfiguration

I believe that I was born a mystic. I do not believe that I am alone in that. When I talk with those who have either tried to live a life of spirit or those rare ones who do so, they talk of their early lives in similar ways. By mystic I mean merely that when I was a child, I experienced things without the prejudice of the materialistic worldview. I saw things and felt things that I could not explain rationally—and didn't know I needed to. Of course.

Now, in these elder years, the same is true. After all of my education and all of my journeys into the scientific world, I still experience the transcendent, the mysterious, the awesome, and awful, and I try not to search for explanations.

I did make that search for years. That was my conditioning, but thanks to over twenty years of Twelve Step work and nearly as many of a mystical practice, I have, for the most part, stopped looking. When I am able to stop, I find what I have been looking for. When I hear the song that says, "I still haven't found what I'm looking for," I want to say, "Stop looking!"

What I never looked for was God. I was and I remain indifferent. What I didn't know was that I was, in fact, looking for the divine and the manifestations and teachings of the divine, the ineffable.

When I stopped drinking and began to recover, I was faced with a concretized God that made me deeply uncomfortable and, like some of my friends, I moved into an Eastern religious practice where there was no talk of God. I admit now that I went there in reaction to, rather than in search of. So I remained attached to a God I didn't believe in.

And then I stopped "doing" anything and learned to just sit in meditation.

When I began this book, it became clear that I needed to survey my past, to see it through my aging eyes instead of the youthful and cynical ones I first brought to that process many decades before.

The revelations have been astonishing. I see now concrete examples of my fascination with the divine, from many years back. I would sit in a swing with my cousin Nita Nell and we would look at the evening skies and we would see things moving there, great forms, human, animal, and other.

When I rode my horse, I was one with that animal. When I jumped out of (perfectly good) airplanes, for pay, I was momentarily, at least, terrified into a few seconds of mindlessness.

The list goes on and on. What is true is that I was born a mystic but that it took every step I have taken, faulty, crooked, and staggering, to get to the point where I could realize the divine, and say, to you, "I was born a mystic," without embarrassment. I had to have this distance and the experience of age to see what has been in front of me all along. I am not separate. From you, from God, from other. And—and—the moment I name God, I kill God. I have no names for God any longer. God is not concretized; God is, in fact, not God.

I drank for the first time when I was fourteen. I drank for the last time, I believe, when I was forty-two. In those in-between years, I was living in a world of greed and anger and folly, and yet, all along, there dwelt in me a man of compassion and wisdom and awakening. I nearly drowned him, but not too long ago, he finally found his way to the surface.

Let me be clear. I do not have faith or belief. I have conviction, based on experience that I didn't ask for and hard work I barely remember doing, that there is a power greater than myself, which dwells within me and which surrounds me at every moment. I breathe that power in. I breathe it out.

It was not always such. I came close to death on three occasions while I was drinking and once after I sobered up. I was reckless in my affections, and I was careless in discharging the simplest of my tasks. I didn't amount to much, and I lost track of my life and times, but I kept on ticking. I have no regrets.

Now, older, I am shedding the need to define anything and remain open and ready to experience the reality of this power some call God.

Right before my mother died, I told her that I knew I had been a real son of a bitch for many years and that I was sorry. She said, "When I see you now, I know it was worth it." She wouldn't let it rest though, typical for her. So she went on and said, "And you were a real son of a bitch for many years."

Sandpaper for the ego.

It has taken every moment of my life thus far to bring me to this moment. It has required years of drinking and drugging, additional years of yearning and folly, the moments of joy and the moments of despair to build this patchwork life I inhabit, gratefully.

Darkness. Light.

Without that, no this.

This is because that was.

Ah, and to know that?

That's the booby prize. I have *known* such things for years, proud of my learning. More folly, and it was all I knew to do, to know. The great masters say that it is in unlearning that we awaken. I had to "let go of [my] old ideas" in order to live without fixed beliefs. I don't regret a moment of those years of delusion, and I am grateful to have seen a break in the clouds.

It happened as such things always do. Very slowly and all at once, and it was all beneath the level of consciousness. These brews ferment in the darkest place.

On June 24, 1984, I had a profound spiritual experience. It worked, as I later learned such events often do, at depth.

There was no white light, no thrills, and no transportation into blissful states of nirvana, heaven, or emptiness. I didn't notice it at all, and yet everything changed. I can feel that moment only in retrospect through mere intellectual recall, always faulty, often a lie. That morning everything was ordinary, and everything, that day, was a manifestation of Grace. I experienced a complete shift of the ground of my being. At one moment, with a glass of brandy in my hand and an open beer can on the table in front of me, at 8:30 in the morning, I was one way. A moment later, I was another. I still had my same small apartment on the

Upper East Side of Manhattan. I had my same job, my friends were still all gone, and I had my same little pile of books and the same aging yogurt in my small refrigerator and the same irritating ring around my bathtub, impervious to Ajax.

That moment later, I poured out the brandy and the beer, tossed the beer can in the trash, put the brandy glass in the sink, and had no desire to drink alcohol, at all. The compulsion that ran me for nearly three decades was gone. I was like that, and then I was like this.

In that instant when ordinary mind touches true mind, all ambiguity evaporates. Small self encounters Self, the pilgrim meets God, the mind of darkness is bathed in the mind of light, I is consumed in Thou, and confusion is gone. "I must drink alcohol" morphs to "I won't drink alcohol" morphs to "I can't drink alcohol" morphs to "I don't drink alcohol." One breath in, one breath out—total and irrevocable awareness of the truth. The beast steps aside and the spirit is revealed, as vulnerable and courageous as a newborn. And, me, Bill Alexander, editor, father, son, lover, failed actor, and bookworm? I just sat there, unaware of anything that had just happened, but without the thirst that had consumed me.

It was not the first such experience in my life of forty-two years at that time, nor was it to be the last in the twenty-three years since, and my conviction is that there are more awakenings yet to come.

I'm sixty-five at this writing and just as uncertain about what happened that day as I was unconscious about it then.

But I know this much now.

My greatest hidden fear has always been of annihilation. If I wasn't careful, I would disappear entirely. If I gave myself in love, I would lose my identity. If I became a "team player," then where would I be? I would lose my identity. I had to control everything carefully. I had to control the lives of my stepchildren so that they would do what they should. I had to control my feelings or I would be annihilated, my identity would disappear. My identity defined me. I was—an alcoholic! There! Now I could belong to a group that, for some, subtly reinforced the folly of separation. I was identified with my illness, and for many years I would not let that go.

I am grateful now for those years of addiction and folly. The end of my drinking and my drugging was hardly the end of my folly. At times, my so-called recovery merely encouraged folly. But all of it allowed me to get to this very spot.

Over the years that followed that day, I had a connected string of experiences of what I see now as glimpses of the absolute, of the face of God, of the truth of the teachings of the Buddha, all such teachings being simply this: There is no separation. I knew that, but I had not made it real. The knowledge of no separation was not incarnate, not actual, but merely a useful intellectual exercise.

How do I tell you of the divinity of being lifted into the stars, sitting on the edge of a cow pasture in a high Himalayan valley? How can I show you, in mere words, what it was like to be sitting on the end of a pier in a nighttime lake, laced with moonlight, and to sense only the lake and the moon, observer gone? There's not a way to say to you, "I saw the face of God standing at the corner of Sixty-seventh Street and Lexington Avenue in New York City," without you thinking I should be examined by a psychiatrist, is there? Or that, just standing in front of a group of other drunks, I felt the separation fall away, if only for a moment. How do I tell you that? I sat with a Zen master and asked how, as a Christian and, more challenging yet, an Episcopalian, I could ever see the Buddha Way, through all those little teaching stories, called koans, that he pestered me with. He said, "As Buddha, when you see through the koan, you will see the face of God." How can I show you that he was right? Face? God? Buddha?

These are words. I heard a teacher say once, "Thing is think." True. The moment I name it, I limit it. Who am I to say, "Look, an eagle!" I saw these things, nonetheless, and many more, but until I began to write this book and to take an entirely new journey through my life to date, I didn't see that they were of a cloth. I stood apart. I suffered from the "paralysis of analysis," and all the time, the divine inhabited me, waiting.

So I can't tell you. That same old master who pointed his finger at God for me once shouted, "Don't tell me, show me."

# Communion

The experience of the divine does not require distant pastures in great mountains, nor the roar of traffic and a brief hallucination in a large city. I didn't have to sit alone on that pier in moonlight to see God. It only happens one way, for this old drunk.

In communion.

Nothing changed, and yet the work of the final opening could begin. I still lived in Florida, I still missed and loved my son, in school in Massachusetts, and I still didn't have enough money, sex, or power. But it was beginning not to matter, all of that.

Now I want to tell you about communion and love—and annihilation.

A dear woman friend of many years and I had dinner one night. I think that if I had listened, I might have heard the pipes of Pan playing in the hills around that little restaurant where we ate good beef and talked about what we were both feeling, after so many years. We drove back to my place. I kissed her goodnight, but our night couldn't end there. Inside, standing up, fully clothed, I held her and she me, both of us with unexpected abandon, as closely as two people have ever held each other. That ancient fear of annihilation surfaced at once, as it always does in such circumstances for me, and I became "loverboy," aloof, a show-off, a performer in the groves of Pan.

Then there was an unspoken message from her, from deep within her body, which traveled the miniscule distance to my body, my heart, and the message said, "You don't have to do that."

I went from loverboy to Lover, in that instant, and there, there, was the communion of the flesh. We were at each other's altars. The altar of the wedding of flesh and spirit. The communion of the body and the blood is actualized, for me, only with other, however other is perceived. I was flesh and blood, one vessel. The holy communion is the reality of no separation.

I had always been the distant one, the performance artist in the sack, arrogant and proud, flying away at the whisper of true love, the love without masks or artifice. I know, from subsequent conversations with my men friends, that they were the same. And what about my aging friends, the guys my age? They've turned their backs on sex. "Don't need that. I just go to the mall, do some shopping, and then sit in the food court and look at the jiggles."

I think I had no greater gate to pass through than the opening to eroto-spiritual connection. I'm not alone. In the West, particularly, fascinated and seduced by supple youth and pornographic advertisements and hatred of sex, and fear of intimate connection, we rarely approach the hidden door, completely naked and unmasked. I had to lose that playboy body and mentality, and I had to be willing to die to the flesh to enter that gate. I had to be old and sexually unattractive, to the mind of the marketplace, to enter that gate.

And then it was there, as it had been all along, in this woman. In the divine feminine incarnate. It waited all along until my heart was battered enough to break open.

I think many of my friends and lovers might say they weren't sure it would ever happen. Folly runs deep, after all.

The story I will tell about that moment ends here. But it hasn't ended.

At that moment there was the final crack, the ultimate tear, and my heart broke apart. Now when I write to you, when I speak, when I think, it is from a broken heart. No, not a broken heart, a heart that broke and then, in the crucible of connection, melted into a new, rougher shape, a patchwork of all the old pieces, welded by blood and sorrow and ecstasy. My heart now, this one right here, is irretrievably pierced by the sadness of the world and its beauty and its squalor and its fleeting life, and I find my reality there, in the interpenetration of all those shards. In the Japanese tea ceremony, the cups that are revered are the broken ones. When they are repaired, powdered gold is mixed with the common glue. It is what is broken that lets the light in.

Everything is broken.

I have the heart of an old man. I see the fragile beauty and know like I could never have known before how transient it is; I see the squalor and the pain and know like I could never have known before how transient it is. The joy, too, so fragile that I dare not take it into my hands, for fear I will kill it, like the tiniest of birds. I only pray to participate in the joy, knowing the suffering as well. Like a child, I must have courage to be fully in this world.

But I am not like a child, not really. I have seen too much of the world to ever be that again. But this old man, with his makeshift heart, has learned to look deeply at the joy and to feel deeply the suffering and, on occasion, to feel the beat of the wings of angels as they surround me. The tempo of my heart is ragged, and if I listen to that shattered pulse, I sense, between the beats, the stillness of God. With this broken heart I hear what my damaged ears will never hear. The voice of God, whispering through the scars and the blood.

It was through a broken heart that God finally found a passage and could enter, with grace and tenderness, so gently I did not know she or he was there at first.

I did nothing to deserve this small awakening to the transcendent and I have no explanation of how it happened.

Except this. I was prepared. I don't live meditatively to find enlightenment. I do so in the hope that I will be awake when enlightened insight shows up.

I am not rigid in my beliefs. I think you need to have some years on you to finally get that way. And, I fear, my arrogance is still enough with me that I felt I wanted to tell you about it. But the rigid way? That way, for us older folks, is the precise way to die long before the body gives out.

Just look around.

> *"No confusion within the gate, no dust*
> *my empty home harbors idleness to spare.*
> *Back again, after so long in that trap,*
> *I've returned to all that comes of itself."*
> —T'ao Ch'ien

# Reverie: The Mind of the Hermit

*I'm sitting on the downstairs veranda of my little two-story ma-*
*hogany and tin-roofed native house in the tropics, just on the edge*
*of the jungle. It's just one big open room, this part, with chairs*
*and couches and the kitchen. There's a cigar smoldering on the red*
*china plate I use as an ashtray, and the hot night air carries the*
*sounds of tree frogs and the mysterious guttering of the critters of*
*the jungle, just over there, always out of sight. My bare feet are up*
*on the rail, and I'm wearing a pair of turquoise swim shorts and a*
*stained white tank top, still damp from a late-evening swim in the*
*gulf. I'm not wearing my store-bought upper molars—rarely do*
*anymore—and my knees are bloody, again, from a spill, again, in the*
*heavy surf. I surf like an old man. Fearless and gawky and silly,*

but I surf. My little CD player is belting out "Sweet Virginia" by the Stones through the big speakers in the rafters ("Got to scrape that shit right off of your shoes"). There's an iced, sweaty bottle of Reed's Ginger Ale on the poured concrete floor by my rocking chair. And there's the scent of coconut, so sexy, from the salve I slather on for this time of night, the hours of the stinging insects.

There is a woman in the kitchen. She is unknown to me in the "real" world, but so very familiar in this world of reverie. It is an open kitchen and she is cooking up the red snapper I caught that day. We trade cooking chores, and when I catch the food, she cooks it. The scent of garlic and fresh hot chili peppers floats out from our little galley kitchen.

I drift. I think of the prayer that Elene Loecher taught me years ago. "Give me the mind of a child and the awesome courage to live that out." Am I doing that? Is that what that old poet T'ao Ch'ien did? I'd like to think that he inhabits me now. Or maybe made room for me, just over the horizon.

"Back again, after so long in that trap"! The world of this and that, getting and having, that I inhabited for so many years.

"All that comes of itself"! The stark reality of what is. I no longer try to control anything. I have arrived at the life of perfect idleness, with no worms devouring my small self, gone, gone beyond, riding the arising and the falling of the world. Content. Perfectly content.

I lean back, screwed-up knees bent, fingers linked behind my head, and continue composing my ongoing elegy, an exercise for *my mind that demands attention from time to time. I don't write anything down anymore. I just enfold myself into the waves of my mind, content to surf them home.*

*I am at peace with the results of my faith. I am home.*

*Ah. I write nothing down, nothing.*

*I'm through writing, you see.*

That jungle home is out there, calling—a message from the hermit within. A jungle home, a woman, endless surf, and quiet nights? In an old man's mind only, maybe, maybe, but I can easily move in. T'ao Ch'ien and his old lady just moved out.

There's another way to look at this reverie, of course. There always are many facets to a message from the hermit. I sat with this one for a few days and I let him speak.

What's it about? Only this. An old man, living a life of simple-hearted contentment, serving the young ones, and finding spiritual and erotic love deeply intertwined. An old man, his heroes all dead but always present to his heart. An old man, returned to things as they are and living as he lived as a child, in awe and wonder. The place, the circumstances, the people? Don't matter. It's the return home, my friend, that's all. My tropical reverie was the truth, told by the hermit, of what it is to be at home. Simplicity, silence, and love. Love. Love, above all, abides. There is always the possibility of love and of home, found again and again until the roots take and fear turns to dust borne on the evening breezes.

I spent most of my life in a place other than home. In my elder years, through surrender and meditation, I have come home to the place I always was and I see it, in its simple beauty, for the first time.

That's my story, anyway. What's yours?

Love,

Bill

## About the Author

William Alexander is a writer and storyteller with no fixed address. He is the author of *Cool Water: Alcoholism, Mindfulness, and Ordinary Recovery* and *Still Waters: Sobriety, Atonement, and Unfolding Enlightenment*. You may contact him through his Web site: www.onefathom.com.